E-MAIL

COMMUNICATE EFFECTIVELY

First Edition

Verna Terminello

English Department, Columbus State Community College

Marcia G. Reed

Performance Consultant, MGR & Associates, Inc.

Terminello and Reed are co-founders of E-mail E-mmunities at www.emailemmunities.com

JOB SKILLS

NETEFFECT SERIES

Prentice
Hall

Upper Saddle River, NJ 07458

Library of Congress Cataloging-in-Publication Data

Terminello, Verna
   E-mail: communicate effectively / Verna Terminello & Marcia G. Reed.
      p.   cm.
   Includes bibliographical references and index.
   ISBN 0-13-041817-X
   1. Electronic mail messages.   I. Reed, Marcia G.   II. Title.

HE7551 .T47 2002
651.7'9—dc21   2002017087

Publisher: *Steve Helba*
Executive Editor: *Elizabeth Sugg*
Editorial Assistant: *Anita Rhodes*
Director of Manufacturing and Production: *Bruce Johnson*
Managing Editor: *Mary Carnis*
Manufacturing Manager: *Ilene Sanford*
Production Liaison: *Brian Hyland*
Production Management: *BookMasters, Inc.*
Design Director: *Cheryl Asherman*
Design Coordinator: *Christopher Weigand*
Marketing Manager: *Tim Peyton*
Printer/Binder: *Von Hoffman–Owensville*
Cover Printer: *Coral Graphics*

Pearson Education LTD.
Pearson Education Australia PTY, Limited
Pearson Education Singapore, Pte. Ltd
Pearson Education North Asia Ltd
Pearson Education Canada, Ltd.
Pearson Educación de Mexico, S.A. de C.V.
Pearson Education—Japan
Pearson Education Malaysia, Pte. Ltd
Pearson Education, Upper Saddle River, New Jersey

10 9 8 7 6 5 4 3 2 1
ISBN 0-13-041817-X

Contents

3

E-mail IS Business Writing: Composing Letters, Memos, and Notes at Work   43

4

Managing the Barrage of E-mail: Using a System to Organize, Process, and Declutter   74

Acknowledgments

Since we began writing *E-mail: Communicate Effectively*, we have a whole new relationship with the Acknowledgments section of a book. We now intimately know the process of birthing a book and turning it over to others to help nurture it into its fullness. Our team helped us transform research, ideas, and experience into a book that makes a greater contribution to our electronic communities' collective conversations. The power of collaboration is magical.

We are blessed to have many gifted, skilled, and generous friends and associates in our lives who were willing to give us sensitive and insightful feedback.

We would like to thank several of our customers in Columbus, Ohio who helped us pilot and refine our content: Sue Wilburn and Brian Ritchie of Children's Hospital, Michele Barregarye of Employers Resource Association, Gerald Mosko and Rita Gallagher of Banner Stamping Company, Carter Young and Julie Willis of OASIS Corporation, Patricia Dove and Chris Pritchard of Cardinal Health, and Mary-Wood Andersen at Worthington Industries.

We would also like to thank Roger W. Smeltzer, Sr., of Gulfstream Aerospace, Dallas, TX for his executive and customer service perspectives on electronic communication. Also in Columbus, Bill Houston at WorldCom contributed his unique wisdom about efficiency and organization in all aspects of work. Karen Houser of Leader Technologies generously contributed her journalistic, management, and hospitality experience to enrich our writings. We also want to express deep appreciation to Irene Ward who is passionate about honoring all people and is excited about the Internet to help connect people who might otherwise be excluded.

We are also grateful for the tireless contributions of our fellow board and forum members of the Central Ohio Chapter of the American Society of Training and Development; Mallard Owen of eBrite, Ltd.; Sheri Bidwell of Connections for Learning; Alex Freytag of Profitworks; and Barbara Balog of Corporate Communications Services.

We especially want to thank Elizabeth Sugg, Leigh Ann Simms, and Tim Peyton of Prentice Hall who supported our vision for this book and helped bring it to the world. Jennifer Welsch of BookMasters, Inc., led our team to edit and polish our manuscript.

Of course, we could not possibly overlook our funny and furry office mates, Sonnie and Paulie Terminello. On days when we got much too serious, they kept us sane and made us laugh. On the home and office front, Rod Terminello provided loving support and grounded, professional advice. His unfailing faith in us has helped us turn our vision into a reality.

We are overjoyed to present the fruits of our collective labor.

Preface

E-*mail: Communicate Effectively* is the result of our work with organizations facing the challenges of communicating in the new millennium. As e-mail use increases, so do performance issues about this still misunderstood communication medium.

In 1999, we formed E-mail E-mmunities, Inc. By conducting ongoing research and by staying up to date with literature and organizations, we have been able to determine individual performance and organizational needs around electronic communications. Our goal is to help build healthy and productive electronic communities through effective and responsible communication.

This book is intended for anyone who uses e-mail at work. It can be used as a self-study guide or as a supplement to training. The book can also be used to teach and coach others.

Chapters 1 through 4 provide a foundation for effective and responsible e-mail use.

- Chapter 1, E-mail: The Good, the Bad, & the Ugly, sets the stage for understanding the advantages and disadvantages of e-mail.

- Chapter 2, Business Netiquette: Being a Good E-mmunity Netizen at Work, presents some simple Internet etiquette guidelines and solutions.

- Chapter 3, E-mail IS Business Writing: Composing Letters, Memos, and Notes at Work, presents simple strategies for writing e-mail.

- Chapter 4, Managing the Barrage of E-mail: Using a System to Organize, Process, and Declutter, presents ways to help you organize, process, and declutter your e-mail.

In Chapter 5, The Heart and Soul of E-service: Using E-mail to Enhance Customer Service, the core skills from the first four chapters are applied to customer service. E-mail has become a key customer service tool, but rarely are we taught to use it to build relationships with internal and external customers. This chapter presents a process for using e-mail to build loyal customer partnerships.

In the appendix, a Style Guide for E-mail: Standards for Effective E-mail Communications, we provide standards and guidelines to help you develop your own professional e-mail style.

To support our ongoing research, we invite you to share your e-mail experiences with us. You can contact us through our Web site at www.emailemmunities.com.

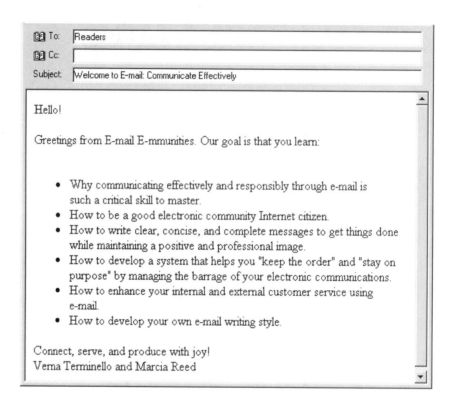

To: Readers
Cc:
Subject: Welcome to E-mail: Communicate Effectively

Hello!

Greetings from E-mail E-mmunities. Our goal is that you learn:

- Why communicating effectively and responsibly through e-mail is such a critical skill to master.
- How to be a good electronic community Internet citizen.
- How to write clear, concise, and complete messages to get things done while maintaining a positive and professional image.
- How to develop a system that helps you "keep the order" and "stay on purpose" by managing the barrage of your electronic communications.
- How to enhance your internal and external customer service using e-mail.
- How to develop your own e-mail writing style.

Connect, serve, and produce with joy!
Verna Terminello and Marcia Reed

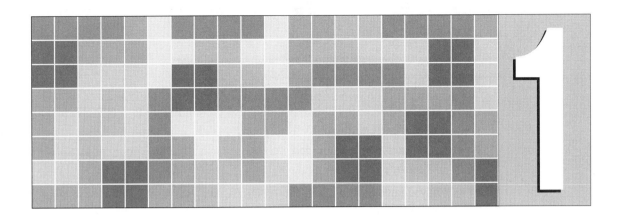

E-mail: The Good, the Bad, & the Ugly

"E-mail can be the greatest communication tool in your organization's history or the greatest curse. What makes it one or the other is the culture that evolves within the organization for using e-mail as a communications tool."

—Ragan's Intranet Report, 1999

WHAT YOU'LL LEARN IN THIS CHAPTER

Goal

- To build awareness of e-mail use and the need to communicate effectively and responsibly

Objectives

As a result of this training, you should be able to:

- Define e-mmunity and state what e-mmunities you belong to
- State why e-mail is mission critical to your job and your organization
- List advantages and disadvantages of using e-mail
- Know when e-mail is the appropriate form of communication to use

---

ASSESS YOUR E-MAIL QUOTIENT (EQ)

Check ☑ *the following statements that cause you concern.*

☐ 1. Are you not using e-mail effectively and efficiently?

☐ 2. Have you ever experienced problems that resulted from misunderstandings or miscommunications through e-mail?

☐ 3. Do you ever feel bombarded with unnecessary, poorly written, or just plain junk e-mail?

☐ 4. Are you not keeping your mailbox tidy, causing your e-mail database to grow out of control?

☐ 5. Have you ever sent questionable e-mail?

☐ 6. Have you ever dashed off e-mail when you were angry at the person you sent the e-mail to?

☐ 7. Have you ever sent e-mail you regretted?

☐ 8. Have you ever sent e-mail and wished you had called or had a face-to-face meeting instead?

☐ 9. Do you ever send e-mail assuming only the recipient will see it?

☐ 10. Do you ever send e-mail that causes confusion and takes several more communications to straighten out?

If you placed a check next to three or more of these questions, you probably need some pointers on communicating effectively and responsibly through e-mail.

Here begins your adventure of discovering why and how to improve your e-mail communications.

E-MAIL IS A MISSION CRITICAL COMPUTER APPLICATION

Electronic communication is here to stay, and its use is increasing rapidly. The global economy is expanding. New technologies are developing at near frenzied rates. The use of the Internet continues to explode. People are connecting more now than ever in history, and *communicating through* **e-mail** *is the most common way people are connecting.*

E-mail is now a **mission critical** *application* of computers everywhere. E-mail is an essential tool for carrying out the mission and goals of an organization. Bill Gates (1999, p. xvii-xviii) characterizes e-mail as central to the life of a business—a "digital nervous system . . . providing a well-integrated flow of information to the right part of the organization at the right time." Gates (1999, p. xix) further explains that this digital nervous system supports the three main corporate functions: commerce, **knowledge management**, and business operations. Employees who perform these functions use e-mail to share files, conduct **e-commerce**, conduct research, collaborate as teams, manage projects, capture knowledge, and provide customer service. If their e-mail servers shut down, the standard operations of their organizations would be paralyzed.

> "*Acting responsibly and following general customs allows users to experience a global adventure of open communication, information, and resources which ultimately provides a unique exploration of the electronic frontier called Cyberspace.*"
>
> –Rinaldi, 1995

In nearly all organizational settings, *the ability to use e-mail well has become crucial.* Even in personal communications, people do not have time to waste on e-mail. As e-mail use continues to grow, *the need to communicate effectively and responsibly increases.*

Using e-mail well is actually now a *basic skill* required by many employers, even though seldom listed in job descriptions. As with other basic skills, employees are assumed to have achieved certain competency levels in using e-mail when they start a job.

To be considered competent with e-mail, users should *minimally* be able to:

- Use software applications to perform basic e-mail functions.

- Compose clear, concise, complete, professional messages.

- Use e-mail to further job and organizational functions.

- Comply with the organization's policies and procedures about computer and e-mail use.

- Practice basic **Netiquette** (Internet etiquette).

- Manage the barrage of e-mails.

- Follow generally accepted e-mail standards and adapt these standards according to their **e-mmunities**' (electronic communities) expectations for communication.

The purpose of e-mail is to simplify, streamline, and enhance communications. E-mail should help users be more effective and efficient. Why then is using e-mail causing trouble for some people?

Organizations often experience problems with e-mail because users receive little, if any, formal training on e-mail, except perhaps a short course on their e-mail software application. Many organizations do not even have set policies about e-mail or computer use. Most users learn about e-mail by trial and error or incidentally, learning "by osmosis." These methods are not always sufficient for learning how to use e-mail *effectively and responsibly. This chapter explains why improving e-mail use must be deliberately and consciously pursued.*

E-MAIL HAS ALWAYS BEEN A GOOD THING

> "E-mail 'enables people to circumvent many of the inefficiencies of the office place and the approval process of traditional paper-based communications.'"
>
> –Angell and Heslop, 1994

> "E-mail 'speeds up the decision-making process by providing a forum for replies or clarifications. It also facilitates meeting planning and preparation.'"
>
> –Angell and Heslop, 1994

> "The ability to quickly and easily share a message even with an attachment also makes collaboration with multiple parties straightforward."
>
> –Overly, 1999

Computers have evolved from being mainly computational engines to serving largely as business and interpersonal communication tools. As the catalyst for this change, e-mail introduced conversations that connected humans in unique ways. While this method of communication began informally and was generally used informally, the evolution of e-mail to a mission critical application has necessitated big changes in this communication style. Here is how the story goes . . .

When e-mail began, it just sort of happened. It was never deliberately developed as a new technology. Instead, e-mail began more like the discovery of a natural phenomenon (Campbell, 1999).

About 30 years ago, Leonard Kleinrock, a UCLA computer science professor, sent the first e-mail message to a colleague at Stanford University. When the message arrived, the computer crashed.

A few years later, Ray Tomlinson, author of the first e-mail software, sent the first successful message. Tomlinson chose the @ sign as the locator symbol in electronic addresses and launched the digital information revolution (Loftus, 1999). Engineers and scientists eagerly adopted e-mail as their preferred mode of communication with each other.

What actually began "mainly as a way for nerds at UCLA to play Dungeons & Dragons with geeks at MIT" (Loftus, 1999) quickly became an easy, rapid system of communication among the first users of networked computers and eventually the Internet. E-mail was informal—often written without punctuation or capital letters. The first e-mail users often ignored style and grammar and adopted the medium as a fast back and forth communication. Their e-mail messages did not have to comply with business writing conventions. *E-mail was appropriately informal then because the e-mmunities accepted informality as the standard.*

USING E-MAIL HAS INTRODUCED SOME CHALLENGES

E-mail is evolving from its original freewheeling style to a more businesslike professional style, especially when used to communicate at work. Because e-mail is rapidly becoming the most common way people in business communicate, it *must* take on a new style.

E-mail must be thoughtful, reader-friendly, reflect well on the sender, and serve the needs of the recipient. No longer can e-mail messages seem like notes passed back and forth in school. E-mail cannot feel like brain-dumps with the subject line filled in "FYI" (for your information). Although in the past these informal styles were acceptable, users are now getting feedback that a very casual style just does not work.

E-mail is a powerful communication tool but causes nightmares for some users. As e-mail use increases, mailboxes get fuller and fuller. Messages must be written better to be read and acted on quicker. E-mail users must also know how to manage the ever-increasing barrage of e-mail so e-mail does not swallow them up. Instead, users must continue to find new, efficient, purposeful applications of this powerful communication tool. E-mail basics should be mastered or users may feel they are trapped in an e-mail nightmare.

Basic e-mail conventions and policies are still emerging as e-mail use increases. Some savvy e-mail users purposefully set policies and standards in electronic communities they communicate with regularly. However, this practice is not the norm. Users must often intuitively discover what is acceptable or not. This practice can be dangerous and may even leave an individual, group, or entire organization vulnerable to a lawsuit. Setting explicit standards takes time and energy, especially as the use of e-mail and computers evolves and increases. To support efficient, ethical, and legal use of e-mail, organizations should set policies and adopt general standards for electronic communications.

E-mail is a public conversation where image and etiquette are critical. Because people are connecting as never before, their images and the images of their organizations are "on the line." Netiquette guidelines are emerging to help users send the right message. Guidelines about style and use are being adapted from business writing and etiquette conventions. Because e-mail is always evolving and is really a hybrid form of communication, some of the guidelines are still being formed. People must be aware of and practice these guidelines or they may find their e-mail use is troubled.

> "E-mail is the greatest threat since lead dinnerware addled the brains of the Roman aristocracy."
> –Shostak, 1999

> "E-mail 'encourages messaging because it is relatively anonymous. The shy, the introverted and the socially inept can all hunker down before a glowing computer and whisper to the world.'"
> –Shostak, 1999

> "E-mail leaves a trace that is very traceable, printable and anything but private. Real-life e-mail disasters can happen to anyone who doesn't pay close attention to the possible technical and emotional glitches only e-mail can offer."
> –Braddock, 1999

E-MAIL IS A UNIQUE FORM OF COMMUNICATION

E-mail is unlike any other form of communication. It is composed and sent but requires no paper or stamp. E-mail is generally reliable and usually arrives within seconds in the recipient's mailbox. It can be composed easily and sent quickly. Unlike voice mail, the message can be planned and revised instead of made up on the spot.

However, e-mail does not carry the gestures, body language, and visual cues of a face-to-face conversation. E-mail does not even carry the tone or voice inflections of a phone conversation. Sometimes senders write things they would not say in person and tend to be more blunt and direct in e-mails. Then recipients may miss the point: they may "miss-interpret," "miss-conclude," or "miss-understand" the intended message!

> "E-mail is a funny hybrid, something between a phone call (or voicemail) and a letter."
> –Levine and Baroudi, 1994

E-mail is being used today to share information in ways not even imagined by its original users: to post job openings, to share birth and death announcements; and to share recipes, jokes, pictures, and files. Who knew e-mail would *evolve as a way to communicate* effectively with customers and serve a whole array of business functions, such as team and project management? Could anyone have guessed e-mail would become so *central to the well-being of organizations*?

COMMUNICATING BY E-MAIL HAS MANY ADVANTAGES

E-mail, when used effectively and responsibly, is an amazing tool!

E-mail is inexpensive, usually reliable, and convenient.

- It connects people and information quickly and easily.

- It keeps information moving without having to schedule a meeting or interrupting someone.

- An e-mail message is prepared more quickly than a letter.

- It is a great way to communicate while on the road.

- E-mail allows users to be flexible. E-mailers do not have to be communicating at the same time or in the same place.

- E-mail used effectively and responsibly can increase productivity, save time, and reduce the costs of long-distance phone calls.

- E-mail saves the time of printing, copying, and distributing information to a number of people.

E-mail documents can be managed.

- E-mail messages can be sent to multiple recipients, forwarded, and even stored in files once cleared from the e-mailbox.

- E-mail can be drafted carefully and purposefully to make sure the message is clear, correct, and concise.

- E-mail programs can be integrated with other office systems.

- E-mail leaves a formal record or backup documentation.

E-mail is an effective time management tool.

- E-mail can be composed, sent, managed, read, and responded to when users have time. Users do not have to be interrupted to communicate until they are ready to do e-mail.

- E-mail can reduce telephone tag.

- E-mail messages, when left in a mailbox for review, act as great reminders.

E-mail is a collaboration tool.

- It connects people across time zones and in different areas of the world.

- E-mail flattens organizational structures because people are apt to e-mail each other regardless of position or rank. Employees look pretty much the same electronically. With e-mail, everyone has access to each other, and communication becomes more lateral.

- E-mail can speed up a decision-making process by connecting people and information quickly and easily.

- E-mail allows more people to be included in expressing their opinions.

- E-mail's quick turnaround allows users to correct mistakes or clarify information.

E-mail has many applications.

E-mail can be used to:

- enhance customer service

- manage projects

- manage performance

- plan meetings

- send newsletters

- conduct surveys

- collect and report data

- improve morale

Reflection Activity *E-mail—The Good*

1. Why is e-mail mission critical to your job? To your organization?

2. What are some effective ways you have used e-mail in your organization?

E-MAIL IS A GOOD WAY TO COMMUNICATE—*SOMETIMES*

E-mail is a great way to share information. It is best used at work when:

- Messages have to go to a lot of people quickly.

- Someone cannot be reached by phone.

- Fast turnaround is required.

- The communicators are at different locations and may be in different time zones.

- The users want a written record or **threaded conversation** kept for a **knowledge base** or electronic "**paper trail**."

> *"E-mail can provide employees with an efficient and economical means of communicating among themselves and with customers and vendors—even when the intended recipient is in a remote office, working at home, or traveling."*
> —Overly, 1999

E-MAIL ALSO HAS DISADVANTAGES

E-mail, when not used responsibly, can cause some trouble.

E-mail messages may be misunderstood.

- *Poorly written messages can cause confusion or misunderstandings and may take additional communications (and time) to straighten out.* The following two e-mails inform the recipient that a meeting time and location have been changed. The first message is poorly written and hard to follow. The second message clearly communicates the necessary action, as well as the date, time, and location of the meeting.

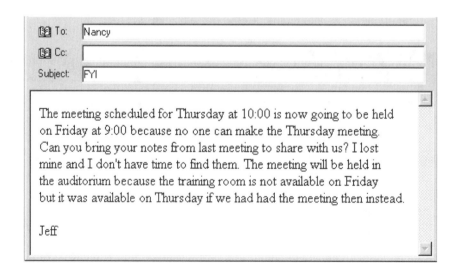

To: Nancy
Cc:
Subject: FYI

The meeting scheduled for Thursday at 10:00 is now going to be held on Friday at 9:00 because no one can make the Thursday meeting. Can you bring your notes from last meeting to share with us? I lost mine and I don't have time to find them. The meeting will be held in the auditorium because the training room is not available on Friday but it was available on Thursday if we had had the meeting then instead.

Jeff

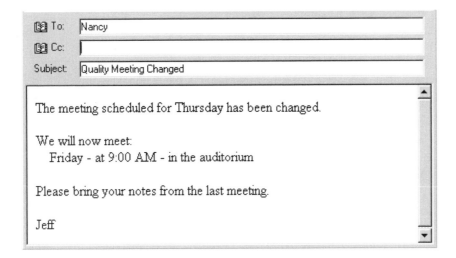

- A *sensitive message's meaning must be negotiated face-to-face or voice-to-voice.* An e-mail message can be misinterpreted or can create bad relations because the voices, gestures, pauses, or other nonverbal cues are lost. The following e-mail message addresses a sensitive issue that would be better handled face-to-face. In an interactive, face-to-face conversation, Marv might discover that Joan did not realize the parking spot was Marv's and is willing to find a new place to park.

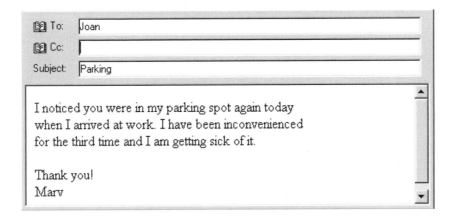

- An *e-mail written without using the proper tone to support the message may be misinterpreted or come across as sarcastic or harsh.* A misinterpreted tone in e-mail can even undermine relationships and create hurt feelings. The tone of Sam's message could be misinterpreted as whining or sarcastic.

> "E-mail can be a disembodied horror, threatening not just privacy and intellectual community but literacy itself."
>
> –Tolson, 1999

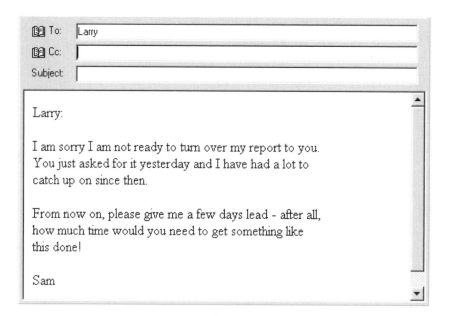

Larry's harsh response is called a flame, or nasty note. Notice how he shouts with capital letters.

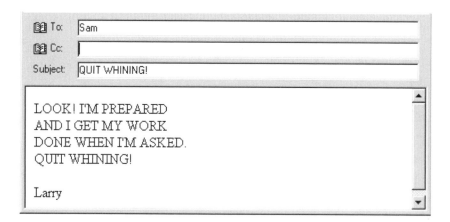

E-mail can feel like a bombardment of messages.

- A long, disorganized message might not be read at all, or the message may be considered bothersome by someone who has to wade through many e-mails daily.

"E-mail is aggressive. It has a built-in, insistent arrogance. Because it arrives more or less instantaneously, the assumption is that you will deal with it quickly."

–Shostak, 1999

- *E-mail that is misused, mismanaged, or nonwork-related may be considered as wasting time and resources, hogging **bandwidth**, and even clogging company databases.* Some organizations monitor employees' e-mail and computer use as a result.

- *Junk e-mail, or **spam**, is a nuisance and an invasion of privacy.* Spam is usually an unwanted solicitation from someone unknown to the recipient. Spam is offensive and costs recipients and service providers online time, bandwidth, space, and aggravation. Spam includes get-rich-quick schemes, links to pornography, software offers, health promotions, and investment information.

To:	Lucky Guy
Cc:	
Subject:	Hello!

Best Casino on the Internet! Do you want to play the slots
and never leave home?
http://www.LasVegasWannabeCasino.com
Bring your credit card and your lucky rabbit's foot and log on.
Low stakes, High winnings!

- *A "**jam**" message, another common form of junk e-mail, comes from a person the recipient knows.* This kind of e-mail can be an even greater nuisance because recipients are seduced into opening e-mail from people they know.

  Jam can include jokes, recipes, pleas for business cards from some elementary school class, and chain letters. Recipients may not only hate getting jam, but they are also often perplexed about how to tell the sender to quit sending the junk e-mails. Novice e-mail users often succumb to the temptation to send or forward junk e-mail to everyone they know. They soon learn as users that they do not appreciate jam at all.

> *Some people send out e-mails to everyone as a way of indicating the importance of what they are writing about. It doesn't always serve the recipient's needs. It is often only for the sender's benefit.*
>
> –Paraphrased from
> Frank Willison
> in Lamb and Peek,
> 1995

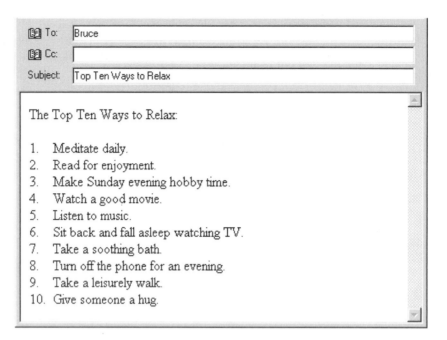

Inappropriate e-mail use can cause legal or ethical concerns.

- *E-mail messages that contain unethical practices or trade secrets can make an organization or individual vulnerable to a lawsuit.*

- *E-mail can create or perpetuate an uncomfortable or even hostile work environment.* If employees are not careful about the kinds of messages they send, the work environment might even be construed as one where bad feelings or discrimination exist. For example:

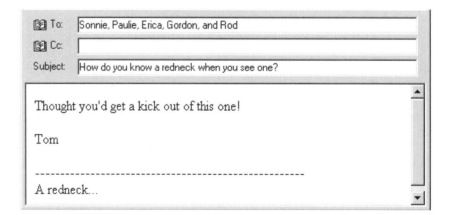

E-jokes that are circulated may be funny to some people and offensive to others. Even if the sender tries to control who the recipients are, employees can share computers or look over shoulders and see messages they were not meant to see. E-mails can be forged or forwarded to unintended recipients as well. E-mail discussing sensitive, confidential issues could wind up in the wrong mailboxes.

- *E-mail is never private.* An e-mail message ALWAYS winds up "on the record"—stored somewhere in a hard drive or server for someone to retrieve even after the user has deleted it.

- *E-mail containing copyrighted materials without proper citation and/or permission could be violating copyright laws.*

E-mail messages may not be consistent with an organization's desired image.

- *An informal message is not usually appropriate in organizational settings and can create a negative image of the sender.* Because e-mail is so quick and easy, users sometimes respond too informally. They may send messages with misspelled or misused words and with punctuation and grammatical errors.

- *E-mail messages may not follow the standard guidelines of Netiquette* and may be considered rude or unprofessional or send the wrong message.

Reflection Activity	*E-mail—The Bad*

What are some problems you have encountered using e-mail?

E-MAIL IS NOT ALWAYS THE BEST WAY TO COMMUNICATE

Although e-mail is a wonderful communication tool, it should not be used when:

- The message is long, complicated, or requires negotiation.

- Questions or information need clarification and discussion.

- The information is confidential, sensitive, requires security, or could be misinterpreted.

- The message is emotionally charged, and really requires tone of voice or conversational feedback to soften the words or negotiate meaning.

- The message is sent to AVOID direct contact with a person, especially if the message is unpleasant and uncomfortable or seems too difficult to say face-to-face.

- The message contains sensitive issues, relays feelings, or attempts to resolve conflict. E-mail can make conflict worse.

■ A response is required quickly, and the receiver is not reading e-mails regularly.

■ The discussion involves several people, and their feedback is required. A teleconference, face-to-face meeting, bulletin board, or discussion group format may be more efficient.

■ The information could be shared more easily another way (such as *talking* to the person in the next office).

OUR E-MMUNITIES HELP US DETERMINE HOW TO COMMUNICATE

E-mail users who communicate regularly with different groups of people have established electronic communities, or e-mmunities. E-mmunities associated with work may include people in professional organizations, vendors, customers, and coworkers. Within the same organization, multiple e-mmunities may exist among team members or coworkers. Of course, e-mmunities can also include people outside work, such as friends, family members, or club members.

E-mmunities establish unwritten and often unconscious conventions about ways they communicate or interact with each other. Some e-mmunities even articulate these guidelines. They may have guidelines about the tones they use, how formal or informal messages are, what response time is expected or considered polite, and what words are used. E-mmunities may even have standards regarding word choice, what kinds of e-mail messages will be tolerated by the group, and even who is admitted to the group.

Responsible e-mail users pay attention to the communication conventions set by the e-mmunities they belong to. If conventions do not exist, some users even take leadership roles to initiate a process to get the e-mmunity to agree upon the standards. They respect the standards and communicate within the guidelines set by the group.

Other responsible e-mail users work with an e-mail buddy inside or outside the e-mmunity to help them compose messages and give feedback.

Reflection Activity	*Getting Help with Your Communications*

1. What e-mmunities do you belong to?

2. What are some of the conventions in your e-mmunity?

3. Where do these conventions come from?

4. Who knows and practices the conventions well? Think of a couple of people who might make good e-mail buddies.

Application Activity	*Setting Up an E-mail Buddy Relationship*

Now that you have thought of a few people to be your e-mail buddy, choose one and invite him or her to partner with you. Take the e-mail buddy pledge to commit to handling challenging correspondences by sharing and editing each other's written work.

Face each other. Put your left hand up and your right hand over your heart and repeat to each other:

"I promise, on my honor, to help my e-mail buddies in their time of need to the best of my abilities. I promise to be positive, cheerful, and gentle when giving feedback and guidance, and most important, I promise to be available."

SOME E-STORIES ARE GETTING UGLY

Irresponsible users of e-mail have gotten themselves and their organizations in some trouble. Here are some examples:

- **Clogged database.** One large telecommunications company has had to close down its server for maintenance because employees were not keeping their mailboxes tidy. The database became so clogged that it could no longer function, and employees could not use their e-mail for hours each time.

- **E-mail evidence seized.** One large software company involved in a major federal lawsuit has had to turn over some e-mail messages that were used as evidence *against the company*.

- **Stolen secrets.** Our national security was threatened when the Chinese stole defense secrets from Los Alamos National Laboratory that were shared by U.S. government personnel via e-mail.

- **Sexual harassment suits.** Companies are being sued for sexual harassment violations because employees send jokes and pictures considered offensive by some people. One large oil company settled for $2.2 million for allowing their e-mail system to be used for "transmitting sexually offensive information."

- **Secret love affairs.** At one company, two coworkers were carrying on a secret love affair. The man e-mailed the woman a message that read, "At last we have found a way we can communicate at work and still have privacy!" He then proceeded to hit the wrong key, and the message was sent to everyone in the office on a distribution list!

> "There have been many instances of love notes, confidential information, and nasty remarks getting broadcast to the wrong people."
>
> –Tittel and Robbins, 1994

- **Digital faux pas.** One manager replied to a party invitation from a friend and tossed in some gossip about a coworker he disliked. He was surprised when a half- dozen other people responded. The manager had accidentally hit "Reply to All" instead of just "Reply," sending his rude comment to many of the office workers, including a number of the coworker's friends. He was too embarrassed to attend the party.

■ **Computer viruses.** Computer viruses are most commonly spread through e-mail. Novice e-mail users who have not yet learned to manage their e-mail may open everything they receive in their mailboxes. This practice is especially dangerous when a virus is making the rounds. The Melissa virus crippled many large organizations for days when it circulated through e-mail. Some users caution never to open e-mails without recognizing and trusting the sender.

And the stories continue . . .

Reflection Activity   *E-mail—The Ugly*

What ugly e-mail stories have you heard about or experienced?

TOOLS & TIPS

Hot Tools & Tips!

The remaining pages in this chapter contain quizzes and job guides such as tips, checklists, and references.

Application Activities

1. Read through the Tiptionary: E-mail Do's and Don'ts. Make a note of the ones you have not heard before.

2. Read through the Savvy Solution for Learning. Choose three actions you can implement to improve your e-mail communications. Create an action list with due dates for each action.

✔	QUICK CHECK*

1. E-mail is a public conversation where image and etiquette are critical.   True or False?

2. Because e-mail is private, it leaves no formal record or back-up documentation after it is sent.

    True or False?

3. Name two ways e-mail is an effective time management tool.

4. Why can the meaning of an e-mail message be misinterpreted?

5. Traditional copyright laws do not apply to information sent through e-mail.   True or False?

6. In business communications, e-mail is expected to be fast and casual.   True or False?

7. E-mail is a good communication tool for hashing out a conflict because people do not have to be uncomfortable facing each other.   True or False?

8. Define *e-mmunity*.

9. Computer viruses are most commonly spread through e-mail.   True or False?

10. Why should you not use sarcasm in an e-mail message?

*Turn to page 153 for answers to the Quick Check.

WOW (Words of Wisdom)	*Using E-mail Effectively and Responsibly*

1. E-mail is never private at work. People share computers and forward messages. Even if you delete an e-mail, it does not just disappear. Trade secrets and confidential information are never safe on e-mail.

2. Poorly written e-mail can create a negative image of the sender and the organization. We are often judged by how we communicate.

3. Do not treat e-mail casually. Proper tone, format, spelling, grammar, and punctuation all count.

4. Know your audience (and potential audiences) before sending an e-mail.

5. Pay attention to the rules of Netiquette (Internet etiquette): avoid spamming, jamming, flaming, and using sarcasm.

6. Manage your e-mail files and do not clog up databases and bog down systems.

7. Learn your e-mmunities' cultures and expectations about e-mail. These guidelines may include: how quickly to respond, how to format a message, and if you are allowed any personal use of your computer at work.

8. Never send confidential or sensitive information by e-mail.

9. Do not use e-mail if you are angry or if a face-to-face communication would be better. See the message through the reader's eyes and think twice before sending.

10. Only send e-mail messages that you would not mind your grandmother seeing or that you would not mind posting on the company bulletin board above the water cooler.

11. Learn your organization's policies and procedures about e-mail use.

12. Remember, e-mail is a mission critical application of the organization and is a powerful communication tool.

SAVVY SOLUTIONS FOR LEARNING INCLUDE

Some savvy solutions for learning how to communicate effectively and responsibly through e-mail

1. Read books, view videos, and visit Web sites about e-mail, including the ones listed in the References section of this chapter and the rest of this book.

2. Find an "expert" on e-mail use and have that person coach and mentor you.

3. Set up a peer-editing team with at least one other person. Practice drafting e-mails and have them received by team members before sending them off.

4. Participate in classes on business writing, Netiquette, how to use e-mail to enhance customer service and team collaboration, and other topics relating to e-mail and electronic communications.

5. Look for training in organizations on how to use e-mail effectively and responsibly:

   - In new hire orientation
   - With e-mail software application training
   - With other business writing or business communication programs
   - As part of time management, customer service, or team training
   - With management or leadership training
   - In train-the-trainer preparation

6. Make sure the organization you represent has a policy on e-mail and computer use. Learn and practice the procedures set by the policy.

7. Help your organization and teams standardize e-mail practices and vocabulary. Communicate these standards in newsletters, intranet postings, or meetings.

8. Create and share examples and templates of well-written e-mail messages that have been used effectively in real communications on the job.

9. Understand the image your organization wants you to project and be sure that your e-mail reflects that image.

10. Make sure you are comfortable in your physical space and you have enough quiet time to stay focused to compose and read your e-mail. Also make sure you have an ergonomically friendly desk, keyboard, and mouse.

11. Make sure you have the tools you need to send and receive e-mail. Do you have and know how to use the hardware and software? Do you know how to use your e-mail software features, such as how to attach a file or route an e-mail?

12. Become an advocate of good e-mail practices by demonstrating how e-mail can save time, avoid trouble, and enhance communications. Show how improving e-mail practices can be part of a quality initiative or a way to reduce operating costs.

13. Help your team members manage their e-mail by using effective time and information management strategies.

14. Obtain or create job aids to help you remember key points about e-mail use. The Words of Wisdom and Tiptionaries in this book are good examples of e-mail job aids.

Tiptionary	*E-mail Do's and Don'ts*

- ☐ Do consider privacy: yours, the recipient's, and the organization's, and the sensitivity of your message's content.

- ☐ Don't "dash off" a first draft and send it too quickly.

- ☐ Do use the same considerations you use when writing a memo, plus.

- ☐ Don't shout with capital letters, flame, or be sarcastic.

- ☐ Don't assume everyone has the same software and can open your message or attached files and see the information the same way you sent it.

- ☐ Don't use e-mail if the message is confidential, unpleasant, may be misunderstood, or requires an immediate response.

- ☐ Don't send junk mail, junk news, advertisements, chain letters, jokes, or anything not necessary.

- ☐ Do remember: People who read lots of mail can be irritated by extra messages or even extra paragraphs.

Key Terms

Bandwidth

Database

E-commerce

E-mail

E-mmunity

Jam

Knowledge base

Knowledge management

Mission critical

Netiquette

Paper trail

Spam

Threaded conversation

References

Adler, J. (1998, November 23). When e-mail bites back. *Newsweek*, 45–46.

Angell, D. and Heslop, B. (1994). *The elements of e-mail style*. Reading, PA: Addison-Wesley Publishing Company.

Braddock, P. (1999). E-mail can result in painful emotional glitches. *New York Times Syndicate*. Available: nytsyn.com/IMDS%7CCND7%7Cread%7C/home/content/users/imds/feeds/nytsyn/.../93 [1999, January 13].

Campbell, T. (1999). The first e-mail message. *PreText Magazine*. Available: www.pretext.com/mar98/features/story2.htm [1999, February 9].

Fastrak Consulting. (1999). Know when to use e-mail. *Features from Fastrak Consulting*. Available: www.fastrak-consulting.uk/tactix/Features/e-mail/mail03.htm [1999, October 15].

Flynn, N. and Flynn, T. (1998). *Writing effective e-mail*. Menlo Park, CA: Crisp Publications, Inc.

Gates, B. (1999). *Business @ the speed of thought*. New York: Warner Books.

Harnack, A. and Kleppinger, E. (1997). *Online!* New York: St. Martin's Press.

Lamb, L. and Peek, J. (1995). *Using e-mail effectively*. Sebastopol, CA: O'Reilly & Associates, Inc.

Levine, J. R. and Baroudi, C. (1994). *The internet for dummies*, 2nd ed. Foster City, CA: IDG Books Worldwide, Inc.

Loftus, M. (1999, March 22). Great moments in e-mail history. *U.S. News*. Available: www.usnews.com/usnews/issue/990322/22hist.htm [1999, March 24].

McKim, G. W. (1996). *Internet research companion*. Indianapolis, IN: Que Education & Training.

McKinnon, W. (1999). *Complete guide to e-mail*. Nepean, Ontario, Canada: Ryshell Books.

Overly, M. R. (1999). *e-policy*. New York: AMACOM.

Quick, R. (1999, January 14). An infinite number of monkeys mistype some of their e-mail. *The Wall Street Journal*, pp. A1, A10.

Shea, V. (1994). *Netiquette*. San Francisco: Albion Books.

Shostak, S. (1999, January 18). You call this progress? *Newsweek*, 16.

Software publishers association issues e-mail guidelines. (1997, August 1). In *Ragan's Intranet Report*. Available: www.ragan.com/html/main.cgi?sub=180&bum=0&maga=&reach=2685&base=story&ma= IR [1999, March 9].

Tittel, E. and Robbins, M. (1994). *E-mail essentials*. Boston: Academic Press.

Tolson, J. (1999, March 22). The life of the mind goes digital. *U.S. News*. Available: www.usnews.com/usnews/issue/990322/22mind.htm [1999, March 24].

Tunstall, J. (1999). *Better, faster e-mail*. Sydney, Australia: Allen and Unwin.

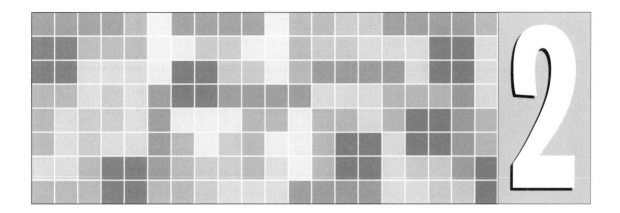

Business Netiquette: Being a Good E-mmunity Netizen at Work

"I prefer commencing with the consideration of an effect."

–Edgar Allan Poe

WHAT YOU'LL LEARN IN THIS CHAPTER

Goal

- To present simple Netiquette (Internet etiquette) guidelines and solutions

Objectives

As a result of this training, you should be able to:

- Define Netiquette and Netizen
- State why Netiquette is so important
- List practices for each of the six Netiquette guidelines

ASSESS YOUR NETIQUETTE E-MAIL QUOTIENT (EQ)

Check ☑ the following statements that describe your use of e-mail.

☐ 1. Do you ever send notes without stopping to think about what, to whom, or why you write to or cc (copy) someone?

☐ 2. Do you ever "jam" people by e-mailing chain letters, top-10 lists, virus warning hoaxes, jokes, or inspirational messages?

☐ 3. Do you *worry or feel guilty* when you do not forward jam?

☐ 4. Do you ever use the cc list as a "power play" by including people on the list to impress them or to impress others?

☐ 5. Have you ever committed the e-version of road rage and flamed (sent a "nasty-gram" to) someone?

☐ 6. Have you ever used jargon, **e-lingo**, acronyms, or **emoticons** (smiley faces that are supposed to express emotion) in your business e-mail messages?

☐ 7. Have you ever sent a **"fatty file"** the recipient could not open? Have you ever bogged down your system or theirs?

☐ 8. Have you ever suffered from **"shortness syndrome"** and sent a message without any context?

☐ 9. Did you ever get annoyed at someone for not responding to an e-mail message and find out they were off work?

☐ 10. Have you ever read anyone's e-mail without permission?

If you placed a check next to three or more of these questions, you probably need some pointers on practicing good Netiquette. Then you can e-mail with the professionalism, efficiency, grace, and charm you use to perform your other job duties.

Here begins your adventure to becoming a good e-mmunity Netizen.

E-MAIL IS THE MOST IMPORTANT WAY WE CONNECT AT WORK

E-mail is a mission critical application of computers. Through e-mail, people are connecting more than ever before. E-mail connects people inside and outside an organization: coworkers, customers, and vendors. E-mail helps teams collaborate and manage projects, enhance sales and customer service, and facilitate communications, transcending time zones and geographic locations.

Most users have never been formally introduced to guidelines about *any* kind of business communications, including how to use e-mail. E-mail requires users to put thoughts "on the line," sending messages for the world to see as never before. Users have to deal with receiving and managing a constantly growing barrage of messages.

Because e-mail is still a relatively new business communication tool, conventions about its use are still evolving. As the technologies change and the applications of electronic communication evolve, so will the standards. In spite of all this change and evolution, how does an e-mail user present a positive image, make better connections, and use e-mail to get things done effectively and efficiently?

Good manners are still a foundation for being effective and responsible communicators

Even though new technologies are evolving and constantly changing the ways we communicate electronically, proper etiquette is still key to effective communication. People who communicate with consideration and respect are heard and not shut down. E-mail's uniqueness requires specific kinds of consideration. *This chapter presents some simple guidelines and practices to help users communicate effectively and responsibly through e-mail.*

NETIQUETTE GUIDELINES HELP USERS BECOME GOOD E-MMUNITY NETIZENS AT WORK

Because of the unique nature of communicating through e-mail, users should follow Netiquette guidelines. Netiquette is the etiquette originally conceived to guide people communicating on the Internet or whenever visiting **cyberspace**. Now, Netiquette includes guidelines for using e-mail in any setting.

Some e-mmunities (electronic communities) set their own guidelines about acceptable ways to communicate. So some e-mail users may already know how to communicate politely. But even if an e-mmunity's guidelines are not established, good **Netizens** (Internet citizens) practice Netiquette anyway!

> *"Definition of **effective**: 'Having the intended or expected effect; serving the purpose.'"*
>
> –The American Heritage Dictionary of the English Language, 1992

> *"Look at the word* **responsibility**—*'response-ability'—the ability to choose your response. Highly proactive people recognize that responsibility. They do not blame circumstances, conditions, or conditioning for their behavior. Their behavior is a product of their own conscious choice, based on values, rather than a product of their conditions, based on feelings."*
>
> –Covey, 1989

> *"Cyberspace contains many different cultures, which some writers have called 'virtual communities.' Each of these communities has its own rules and customs. But many rules apply throughout almost all of Cyberspace.... 'Netiquette' is the etiquette of Cyberspace."*
>
> –Shea, 1994

USING E-MAIL CAN BE GOOD, BAD, OR UGLY

Until users understand that e-mail requires Netiquette, this critical form of business communication may continue to cause problems. In addition to all the advantages of using e-mail, this communication channel can have a negative and even an ugly side.

E-mail is a great way to communicate quickly, easily, and inexpensively. E-mail is flexible and can reach someone who is not available by phone. It is also an effective way to communicate with more than one person. The sender does not have to worry about time or geographical differences. E-mail can be sent and received at the sender's and recipient's convenience.

Another advantage of using e-mail is that the message provides a written record of a communication—an electronic "paper trail" that can be accessed for follow-up actions. Using e-mail also allows senders to *think before they write* to make sure they consider carefully what the message contains, how the message is written, and to whom the message is sent.

As users find more innovative uses for e-mail, they also set themselves up for more misuses and abuses. Because e-mail is so quick and easy, users may find themselves in situations where they may not be particularly polite, careful, thoughtful, or effective. The more they use e-mail, the more they require Netiquette.

BECAUSE E-MAIL IS UNIQUE, USERS MUST BE ESPECIALLY CAREFUL

"Blasko's Law: Courtesy and good taste are inversely proportional to the distribution of computers in a society."

–Blasko, 1999

"The Internet gives you the ability to insult thousands—perhaps millions—of people at the speed of light. The good news, though, is that it also gives you a fast and almost painless way to apologize and make amends—and doing so is excellent Netiquette."

–Wagner, 1999

Communicating through e-mail is different from any other way people have been used to communicating at work. E-mail does not carry the gestures, body language, and visual cues of a face-to-face conversation. E-mail does not even carry the voice tone or inflections of a phone conversation. Many users mistakenly think e-mail messages should be more informal and relaxed than paper equivalents of memos and business letters.

Senders often write things they would not say to a person or would not write in an official interoffice memo. Users tend to be more blunt or direct in e-mail. Then recipients may miss the point: they could misinterpret, misconclude, or misunderstand the intended message.

E-mail recipients may even feel violated when people send unwanted or unsolicited messages and enter their computer mailbox without asking permission. Unsolicited messages include "flames," "spam," and "jam."

Some users unfortunately think they are distanced from the person they communicate with through e-mail and resort to sending **flames** or **"nasty grams."** Some experts propose that flaming is equivalent to road rage syndrome because e-mail users may not remember they are communicating with a real person. Like road rage, a machine is positioned between people, and users may hide behind the machine.

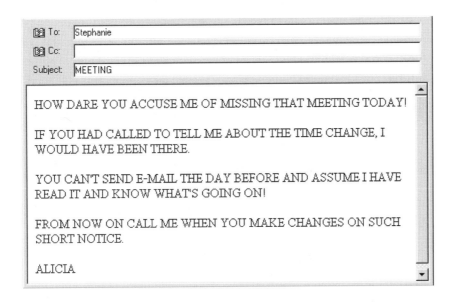

Receiving *spam* is another growing problem with e-mail. Every time someone logs onto the Internet to check for incoming e-mail messages or to send e-mail out, the mailbox can potentially receive spam. Spam, the World Wide Web's version of junk mail, is a nuisance.

Spam is distracting, and the recipient usually goes through several steps to get rid of the message from the mailbox:

1. The recipient reads the return address and decides whether or not to open and read the message or just to delete it.

2. Some recipients get angry and try to flame the sender. They return the message with a nasty gram that somewhere includes the instruction to REMOVE the recipient's name and e-mail address from the spammer's mailing list.

3. Often, the e-mail comes back labeled "Undeliverable," which frustrates the recipient more. The recipient's temper flares, and this *unproductive time* becomes a waste of even more energy. To make matters worse, some e-mail systems automatically add the spammer's address to an address book once they have been sent e-mail. Now *the address entry has to be deleted,* and *spammers know they used a valid address.*

Jam is junk mail users receive from people they know. (Jam has also been referred to as "fram," or friendly spam.) Novice users tend to send jam, just because they can. Many jam spreaders have not used e-mail long enough to be on the receiving end of jam overload. Jam can include: jokes, recipes, pleas for business cards from some elementary school class, and chain letters. Recipients may not only hate getting jam, but they are also often perplexed about how to tell the sender to quit sending the junk e-mails.

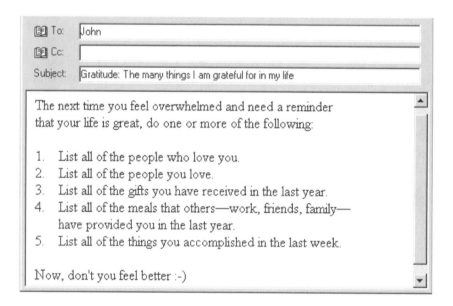

Disregard for the proper use of e-mail can create a whole host of problems.

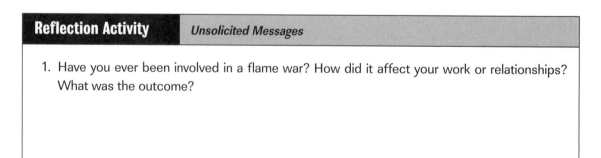

Reflection Activity   *Unsolicited Messages*

1. Have you ever been involved in a flame war? How did it affect your work or relationships? What was the outcome?

2. Do you ever receive spam? What have you done to cut down on spam?

3. Do you ever receive jam? From whom? What have you done to cut down on jam?

E-MAIL BLUNDERS ARE BECOMING ALL TOO COMMON

Very few organizations provide adequate training on how to use e-mail. As a result, users have had to make up their own rules regarding how to communicate. Astute users have taken cues from the people they communicate with regularly (their e-mmunities). Some users have even established their own written guidelines from feedback they get from the e-mmunities they belong to.

> *"Living in an Information Age has profoundly altered our lives, and those who fail to recognize that the rules of information design are changing will find themselves left behind."*
> –Wurman, 2001

But some users have committed serious blunders using e-mail, often unintentionally. Mistakes causing misunderstandings, wasted time, even network downtime and legal action have already threatened individuals and organizations. The threats keep growing as e-mail use becomes more widespread. Here are some examples:

- **Irresponsible performance management.** At one large utility company, managers discussed someone's poor work performance over e-mail. One of the corporate attorneys, who happened to read the e-mails, had to intervene. The e-mail messages could be seized as legal evidence if the named employee filed a grievance against the organization. Proper decorum and good sense say e-mail should not be used to discuss sensitive information.

- **Rude memos.** One provider of human resources services complains that her boss e-mails her from another office regularly. He writes in all capital letters and in red ink. She says she can't get past those style issues to read his messages without being offended.

> *"For some of us, e-mail seems to unleash demons that wouldn't dare drag their cloven feet across a sheet of real paper."*
> –Blasko, 1999

- **Reactive feedback.** At a large publishing company, a newly hired sales rep was confused about her commission structure. When she e-mailed her supervisor for clarification, he lost his temper and YELLED at her, writing some words in all capital letters. He also used quotation marks and underlining to emphasize his frustration. He used what she read as sarcasm and a demeaning tone to belittle her. To make matters worse, he copied the e-mail to five other people. Not only did he not communicate the information well to the rep, the supervisor lost credibility in her eyes and perhaps in the eyes of his supervisors, who soon heard of the infamous e-mail. The next day, he wrote her an apology to try to clear up the issues, and he had to copy the same five people to make the apology public.

> "E-mail has become an incessant distraction, a nonstop obligation and a sure source of stress anxiety. I expect that a public statement by the surgeon general is in the offing."
>
> –Shostak, 1999

- **Insensitive posting.** At a large research organization, an e-mail message was sent to employees regarding the death of a retired employee. Many of the e-mail recipients were offended that e-mail was used to post an obituary.

ONE WAY TO AVOID PROBLEMS IS TO LEARN WHAT GOOD NETIQUETTE IS

Netiquette, the good manners practiced when visiting cyberspace and maintaining civility in electronic communities, should be present in all electronic communications. Some experts have cautioned that Netiquette is more a set of guidelines than rules because of the importance of preserving and honoring the nature of free speech on the Internet.

Some progressive organizations have developed policies and standards for employees regarding Internet use. Some of these standards have been adapted from the already accepted polite ways we know about how to interact in face-to-face communications.

In addition to sending and receiving e-mail, when e-mmunities set Netiquette guidelines for electronic communication, they usually have included how to:

- post messages to online services
- participate in **chat room** discussions, **newsgroups**, or **listservs**.

These guidelines are generally enforced by other members of the e-mmunity, who often object if someone deviates from the standards of Netiquette set forth by the group. Sometimes they don't express their objections, but their judgment taints the communication. Even though only e-mail Netiquette is discussed in this book, many of the same guidelines apply to all forms of electronic communications.

NETIQUETTE IS IMPORTANT BECAUSE E-MAIL IS NEVER PRIVATE

> "... e-mail is like an electronic postcard; messages can be read by anyone who comes in contact with them."
>
> –Overly, 1999

Remember, e-mail is never private at work. E-mail messages *always* wind up "on the record"—stored somewhere in a hard drive or server for someone to retrieve even after the user has deleted them and thinks they are gone.

Many people share office space and computers and can read, retrieve, forward, and even forge messages. Just because a message is deleted, it does not *really* disappear. So sensitive, confidential, or embarrassing information could end up in the wrong mailboxes or be read by the wrong recipients, even unintentionally.

At work, users must be careful to practice good common sense and Netiquette, just as they would practice good manners in any business context. Using e-mail at work is still part of doing a job.

RESPONSIBLE NETIZENS PRACTICE RESPONSIBLE NETIZENSHIP

E-mmunity Netizens, or Internet citizens, come together for a purpose. They most often "connect" to communicate to further actions that get results. Sometimes, they connect to be sociable and build relationships. Regardless of their reasons for connecting, responsible Netizens follow accepted guidelines and practices about how to communicate. By ignoring basic guidelines, people may actually "disconnect." Miscommunications via e-mail can and do exist, and they can be costly. They can cost time, money, even reputations.

> "...I speak here of 'response-ability'—that is, the ability to observe ourselves and others in interaction and to respond to a familiar situation in a new and different way."
>
> –Lerner, 1985

Because users of the Internet are still considered electronic pioneers in an evolving electronic world, Netizens can contribute to the formulation of generally accepted Netiquette guidelines. They can also contribute as good Netizens by demonstrating Netiquette practices and coaching other members of their e-mmunities to do so as well.

At work, Netizens must adhere to the guidelines, practices, and standards of electronic communication emerging from their workplace. Even if the standards have not been outlined by the organization in a policy, responsible Netizens should follow Netiquette guidelines to communicate effectively with coworkers, customers, and vendors.

> "...what matters most is how we respond to what we experience in life."
>
> –Covey, 1989

SIX NETIQUETTE GUIDELINES FOR SAVVY NETIZENS

The following guidelines have emerged from working with organizations to enhance their e-mail communications. These guidelines are explained in detail over the next several pages. To communicate effectively and responsibly at work, savvy Netizens should:

1. Practice the "platinum rule for the new millennium."

2. Put "your best foot forward."

3. Nurture "harmonious connections."

4. Further "e-mmunity action."

5. Travel "the straight and narrow."

6. Clean up the "neighborhood."

PRACTICE THE PLATINUM RULE FOR THE NEW MILLENNIUM

> *"E-mail is the talk radio of the 1990s, (and beyond) and unfortunately, rude opinions from someone with a beef are only a mouse click away."*
>
> –Cooper, 1999

> *"Sometimes it's more tempting to say what you are thinking in writing than on the phone or in person. Don't. It's e-rage and it's not good for your career. If you are agitated, it's better not to communicate at all."*
>
> –Fastrak Consulting, 1999

Always treat others as they would have you treat them. This "platinum rule" is different from the "golden rule," which says "Do unto others as you would have them do unto you."

In the "golden rule," we expect others to conform to our preferences. In the "platinum rule," we flex to their preferences, thus improving relationships and communications.

Responsible e-mmunity Netizens anticipate and honor what other people need in e-mail communications. They have and show consideration for whomever they communicate with. They stop to think how the other person is likely to receive, view, and interpret an e-mail communication from them. They write and format the message so the recipient can read it easily.

They also remember that e-mail is not the appropriate form of communication for sensitive or confrontational issues. These are best handled face-to-face or voice-to-voice. As recipients, they are tolerant and polite in their responses to e-mail—they choose their responses to meet the collective purpose.

Some ways to practice the "platinum rule" in e-mail communications are:

- Prevent misunderstandings and do not give or take offense by e-mail messages.

- Don't send sensitive or confidential information or bad news over e-mail.

- Be careful about using sarcasm in e-mail. Without the face-to-face communications, sarcasm can be viewed as criticism or harsh words.

- Don't challenge a coworker's idea in an e-mail.

- Don't try to hash out conflicts through e-mail.

- Maintain the thread of the conversation by using the reply feature or quotes from the messages you are responding to. When forwarding a message, write a few comments to let the recipient know what is going on. Always supply context and enough information for the reader.

- Be careful about sending attachments. Make sure the recipient has the proper software or files and can open any attachments you send.

> *"The Internet may well trample your feelings if you are sensitive to every perceived wrong. Instead of being quick on the flamethrower trigger, give the benefit of the doubt to your e-mailing friends, family, and business colleagues by assuming the best of their intentions and let most things slide."*
>
> –Wagner, 1999

- Use simple formats in your messages because complex formatting may not appear correctly for all readers.

- Keep the number of characters per line below 80. We never know where the recipient's software might break a line of text. Your message might appear chopped up in strange places if you write a longer line.

- Use upper and lower case letters in e-mail messages. All capital letters are usually seen as shouting.

Reflection Activity   *Platinum Rule for the New Millennium*

Consider your e-mailing experiences on the job. What e-mail practices might you add to ensure that you and your organization practice the "platinum rule for the new millennium?"

PUT YOUR BEST FOOT FORWARD

E-mail messages reflect on users and the organizations they represent. People are judged by how and what they write. Not only do recipients judge the sender's writing skills, but they also look at word choice, tone, and length of the message. Readers may even judge a writer by the way information is organized—especially if the message is disorganized. Fair or not, e-mail messages are always "on the line," and who knows who will see them?

A best practice is to follow this Netiquette guideline and remember:

> *"For centuries, letter writers have pained to get everything from the salutation to the John Hancock as perfect as possible. But the rules for e-mail have yet to be written."*
> –Spring, 1999

- Follow your organization's e-mail standards to project the intended collective image and purpose.

- Treat the composition of an e-mail message as you would a letter on company letterhead. A certain degree of formality is required.

- Pay attention to how you would have addressed a letter and stick to a formal salutation, if appropriate.

- Always use proper grammar, spelling, punctuation, and wording in your e-mail messages.

- Identify yourself at the end of your e-mail by including your name and contact information (your **signature**). If your e-mail system has a signature function, you can create an **e-signature** that will automatically be added at the end of your e-mail.

> *"Your clients measure the quality of your products and services by the image you project in your personal manners, appearance, words, and actions."*
> –Casperson, 1999

- Write concisely so as not to bother people with unnecessary words.

- Be professional and careful about what you say. E-mail is easily forwarded.

Reflection Activity   *Put Your Best Foot Forward*

Consider your e-mailing experiences on the job. What e-mail practices might you add to ensure that you and your organization put "your best foot forward?"

NURTURE HARMONIOUS CONNECTIONS

E-mail allows users to connect as never before. E-mail can enhance or threaten relationships. Building and maintaining trust is critical to harmonious connections. Building and maintaining trust in your relationships with coworkers, customers, and vendors requires socializing, consistency, enthusiasm, acknowledgment, owning problems, individual initiative, predictability, and task focus (Demnitz and Willmore, 1999).

To enhance relationships, practice this Netiquette guideline and:

> *"...make it easy for people to give you what you want or need from them. Seek to connect rather than compete, ask instead of tell, and compliment instead of criticize. You'll end up getting more of what you want, and so will everyone else."*
>
> –Charles, 1999

- Check your e-mail often to see if someone is trying to contact you. Respond to e-mail in a timely manner.

- Only mark an e-mail "urgent" when it truly is not routine.

- Send *personable—not personal*—e-mails. You want to develop good working relationships. So while the purpose of your e-mail is to get the job done, you still need to be friendly and approachable. You do not want to come across as being curt.

- Always identify yourself.

- Follow the chain of command procedures for corresponding with superiors. For example, don't send a complaint via e-mail to the top just because you can.

- Don't get in the habit of using the Bcc: field in your e-mail header to send blind copies of your e-mails. People in the Bcc: field are not listed as recipients in messages received by people in the To: and Cc: field. If recipients know you blind copy other people, they may feel uncomfortable when reading your messages.

> *"No one can hurt you without your consent."*
>
> –Eleanor Roosevelt in Covey, 1989

Reflection Activity   *Nurture Harmonious Connections*

Consider your e-mailing experiences on the job. What e-mail practices might you add to ensure that you and your organization nurture "harmonious connections?"

FURTHER E-MMUNITY ACTION

E-mail is an effective tool for communicating to get things done. Getting things done in a world of information overload is a huge e-mmunity challenge. To further e-mmunity action, astute e-mail users compose and send communications that are "on purpose" and get results. Coworkers, customers, and vendors trust Netizens who stay focused, are consistent, own problems, take individual initiative, and are predictable.

To practice this Netiquette guideline:

- Do not send inappropriate e-mail that contains information regarding personal business, politics, chain letters, and jokes unless the information serves a purpose and is acceptable to the recipient.

- Create an e-mail letterhead for formal proposals, contracts, and offers. Keep the length of the letterhead at three lines or less. Use the letterhead sparingly and only when appropriate to help the recipient(s) focus on the content of the message. Use the letterhead when a message is clearly from your organization and not from you individually.

- Always include your signature at the end of your e-mail message so the recipient does not have to work too hard to find you.

- Send copies of an e-mail message only when necessary.

- Avoid using **acronyms**, smileys, and jargon that may get in the way of the message being understood clearly and quickly.

- Respect the interruption factor and use e-mail *because* it is less intrusive.

Reflection Activity	*Further E-mmunity Action*

Consider your e-mailing experiences on the job. What e-mail practices might you add to ensure that you and your organization further "e-mmunity action?"

TRAVEL THE STRAIGHT AND NARROW

Netiquette addresses some legal, ethical, and just plain common sense issues. Corporate ethics and integrity initiatives should provide guidelines and standards for communicating confidential and sensitive content in a legal and ethical manner. These guidelines suggest practices to avoid spamming, flaming, jamming, violating copyright laws, ignoring security issues, and handling confidential or sensitive issues over e-mail.

> *"...e-mail has become a favorite tool of litigators. E-mail has the frankness of a telephone conversation and the permanence of a written document, and it can be sent to a large number of recipients with little effort."*
>
> *—Goodin, 1999*

An important issue surfacing with the increased use of the Internet is that users of e-mail send information back and forth with little or no regard for *copyright laws*. Not only is information taken from the Internet and e-mailed, sometimes the information is downloaded and printed. Without proper citation and/or permission to reprint, the user could be violating copyright laws.

Information posted on the Internet is protected by the same copyright laws that protect books, software, and other forms of published written communication. If the information is stored illegally on an organization's computer or network, the organization may be liable for a lawsuit.

Another issue concerning appropriate use of e-mail has to do with *security*. Because e-mail is never private, it is also never secure. All information written on e-mail is potentially at risk: user names, passwords, home addresses, phone numbers, family member names, credit card information, account numbers, trade secrets, everything posted! So, e-mail should never be used to discuss confidential, sensitive, or private information.

Some ways to practice Netiquette in e-mail communications while considering the legal, ethical, and just plain common sense issues are:

- Never flame anyone.

- Never send spam. Do not open spam attachments. Do not even open spam messages. Delete them and forget that momentary temper thing.

- Resist the temptation to send jam, especially if the recipient has a low tolerance for e-mail overload.

- Cite all information downloaded, copied, and shared. Give credit to the author and source of the information.

- Use e-mail to send information that can comfortably, ethically, and legally be posted on a bulletin board above the water cooler or can be forwarded to Grandma. E-mail messages should be appropriate for the world to see because the world may actually see them.

- Do not read printed e-mail messages waiting to be picked up from a printer if they are not yours.

Reflection Activity   *Travel the Straight and Narrow*

Consider your e-mailing experiences on the job. What e-mail practices might you add to ensure that you and your organization travel the "straight and narrow?"

CLEAN UP THE NEIGHBORHOOD

Responsible e-mmunity Netizens keep the "neighborhood" clean by managing the barrage of e-mail. They "stay on purpose" and "keep the order" by systematizing, organizing, and decluttering the e-mmunities' collective electronic communications.

Some ways to help clean up the neighborhood include:

- Organize your e-mail daily by reading, sorting, and purging messages.

- Only keep messages in your mailbox that you need to serve as reminders for further actions.

- Regularly delete messages "permanently" from the "deleted" message folder or trash can.

- Keep mailboxes tidy to help keep databases unclogged and e-mail systems running smoothly.

- Write short and simple e-mail messages.

- Don't use e-mail as a way to avoid having face-to-face contact with someone.

- Don't use e-mail when another way to communicate might work better.

- Make sure you do not hog bandwidth. Do not tie up Internet access lines by staying connected too long or monopolize lines by sending "fatty files"

Reflection Activity   *Clean Up the Neighborhood*

Consider your e-mailing experiences on the job. What e-mail practices might you add to ensure that you and your organization clean up the "neighborhood?"

Application Activity   *Action Plan for Netiquette*

It is time for some action planning so when you are on the job you will remember to practice the guidelines. List three to five practices you will apply right away. You can choose all of your practices from one or two of the guidelines you most want to work on. Next to each practice, describe how you will know you accomplished it. What will it look like? How would someone else know you did it? What result should you expect?

Netiquette practice	What result should I expect?

TOOLS & TIPS

Hot Tools & Tips!

The remaining pages in this chapter contain quizzes and job guides such as tips, checklists, and references.

Application Activity

1. Read through the Tiptionary: Questions I Should Ask Myself Before Dashing Off E-mail. Put a star next to each item you do not do automatically. Until you have developed your new Netiquette practices, use the Tiptionary before you send your e-mail.

✔ QUICK CHECK*

1. Before you write an e-mail message think about:
   a. what the message contains
   b. how the message is written
   c. to whom the message is written
   d. all of the above

2. Users tend to be more shy or indirect in e-mail.   True or False?

3. Nasty-grams are also known as _____.

4. _____ is the equivalent of unsolicited junk e-mail.

5. _____ is the junk e-mail you get from someone you know.

6. E-mail mistakes have caused misunderstandings, wasted time, even network down times and legal action threatening individuals and organizations.   True or False?

7. E-mail is a good way to send sensitive, confidential, or embarrassing information so you don't have to talk to the recipient face-to-face.   True or False?

8. One way to "clean up the neighborhood" is to keep your computer screen clean so you can easily read your e-mail.   True or False?

9. You should send copies of e-mail only when absolutely necessary.   True or False?

10. Why should you avoid using acronyms, smileys, and jargon in e-mail?

*Turn to page 154 for answers to the Quick Check.

WOW (Words of Wisdom)	*Guidelines to Business Netiquette*

1. Remember, e-mail is a mission critical application of the organization and is a powerful communication tool.

2. Never before have we had a form of communication as powerful as e-mail, but the potential for miscommunication is also great. Because e-mail is subject to misinterpretation, is public, and is "permanent," miscommunications are more probable and carry greater consequences.

3. E-mail allows senders to think before they write and to choose their responses wisely.

4. Follow your organization's policies and standards for communicating through e-mail.

5. Good manners are still a foundation for being effective and responsible communicators, and good Netizens always follow Netiquette guidelines when sending e-mail.

   - Practice the "platinum rule for the new millennium."
   - Put "your best foot forward."
   - Nurture "harmonious connections."
   - Further "e-mmunity action."
   - Travel "the straight and narrow."
   - Clean up the "neighborhood."

Tiptionary	*Questions I Should Ask Myself Before Dashing Off E-mail*

☐ Is my message easy to read?

☐ Does this message fit the expectations of the receiver?

☐ Does the message suit e-mail or should I communicate the information with a letter, telephone call, or visit to the person instead?

☐ Will I annoy, offend, or confuse anyone with this message?

☐ Was I angry, annoyed, or frustrated when I wrote the message?

☐ Was my message composed with thought and purpose, mindful of the recipient(s), and:

    ☐ Who might read the message?

    ☐ What might their impressions be?

    ☐ How many e-mails do they usually receive, and what will make them read this message?

    ☐ How will the message look when it reaches them?

    ☐ Did I identify myself and make it easy for the recipient to contact me?

    ☐ Will they be able to open and read any attachments?

    ☐ Have I provided enough context for them easily to understand or follow the thread of the message?

    ☐ What is my purpose for sending this e-mail? Will the message seem important to the receiver and meet his/her needs or will it be seen as an annoyance and a waste of time? What action will we further?

Key Terms

Acronym	Flame
Chat room	Listserv
Cyberspace	Nasty gram
E-lingo	Netizen
E-signature	Newsgroup
Emoticon	Shortness syndrome
Fatty file	Signature

References

Casperson, D. M. (1999). *Power etiquette: What you don't know can kill your career*. New York: AMACOM.

Charles, C. L. (1999). *Why is everyone so cranky?* New York: Hyperion.

Cooper, C. (1999, October 13). Flame mailers - go ahead, make my day! *ZDNN*. Available: www.zdnet.com/filters/printerfriendly/0,6061,2352405-2,00.html. [1999, October 17].

Covey, S. R. (1989). *The 7 habits of highly effective people*. New York: Fireside.

Demnitz, C. and Willmore, J. (1999). *Managing virtual teams: Tips and tools for dispersed teaming*. Paper presented at the American Society for Training and Development (ASTD) 1999 International Conference and Exposition, Atlanta, GA.

Goodin, D. (1999, January 21). Journalist's e-mail subpoenaed. *CNET News.com*. Available: news.cnet.com/news/0-1005-200-337663.html?tag= st.ne.1002.srchres.ni [1999, January 23].

Harnack, A. and Kleppinger, E. (1997). *Online!* New York: St. Martin's Press.

Online buffs hit and miss on manners. (1999, March 22). *U.S. News*. Available: www.usnews.com/usnews/issue/990322/22beha.htm [1999, March 3].

Lamb, L. and Peek, J. (1995). *Using e-mail effectively*. Sebastopol, CA: O'Reilly & Associates, Inc.

Lerner, H. (1997). *The dance of anger*. New York: HarperCollins.

Rinaldi, A. (1995, March 1). Internet guidelines and culture. *Florida Atlantic University*. Available: www.fau.edu/netiquette/net/culture.html [1998, November 14].

Shea, V. (1994). *Netiquette*. San Francisco: Albion Books.

Sherwood, K. D. (1998, February 28). E-mail netiquette guidelines. *IEEE*. Available: www.eleccomm.ieee.org/e-mail-netiquette.html [1998, November 14].

Soukhanov, A.H. (Ed.). (1992). *The American heritage dictionary of the English language*, 3rd ed., Boston: Houghton Mifflin Co.

Spring, T. (1999, March 31). The ten commandments of e-mail. *PC WORLD*. Available: cnn.com/TECH/computing/9903/31/commandments.idg/index/html [1999, April 2].

Tittel, E. and Robbins, M. (1994). *E-mail essentials*. Boston: Academic Press.

Tolson, J. (1999, March 22). The life of the mind goes digital. *U.S. News Online*, 3 pages. Available: www.usnews.com/usnews/issue/990322/22mind.htm [1999, March 24].

Tunstall, J. (1999). *Better, faster e-mail*. Sydney, Australia: Allen and Unwin.

Wagner, R. L. (1999). *Road runner guide to cyberspace*. Reston, VA: Citapei Communications.

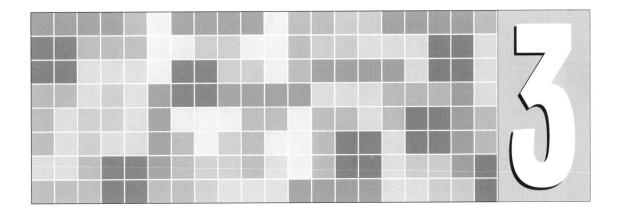

E-mail IS Business Writing: Composing Letters, Memos, and Notes at Work

"Communication is the most important skill in life."

–Stephen R. Covey

WHAT YOU'LL LEARN IN THIS CHAPTER

Goal

- To present some simple strategies for writing effective and responsible e-mail

Objectives

As a result of this training, you should be able to:

- Understand that writing e-mail is a process and know how continuously to improve your own writing processes

■ State some common pitfalls of writing and how to avoid them including:
  ☐ readability
  ☐ word choice
  ☐ audience analysis
  ☐ document design

■ Write clearer, more concise, and correct e-mail messages, memos, and reports

■ Work with an e-mail buddy to compose your e-mail messages

ASSESS YOUR WRITING E-MAIL QUOTIENT (EQ)

Check ☑ the following statements that describe your use of e-mail.

☐ 1. Have you ever experienced problems at work that resulted from misunderstandings or miscommunications through e-mail?

☐ 2. Have you ever sent an e-mail that caused confusion and took at least one more communication to straighten out?

☐ 3. Do you ever send important e-mails without rereading to make sure they make sense?

☐ 4. Have you ever sent an e-mail that covered more than one or two short topics?

☐ 5. Are your e-mails ever longer than a few lines or a few short paragraphs?

☐ 6. Do you ever send negative, sensitive, or confidential information through e-mail?

☐ 7. Do you ever send e-mail without the subject line carefully filled in or filled in with "FYI?"

☐ 8. Do you ever use business jargon, such as "feel free to call me" or "attached please find?"

☐ 9. Do you ever dash off a response to an e-mail without repeating any background information or supplying any context to tie to the original message?

☐ 10. Are you ever in such a hurry that you send e-mails without verifying names, dates, titles, or spellings of people or events mentioned in the messages?

If you placed a check next to three or more of these questions, you probably need some pointers on composing your e-mail.

Here begins your adventure of discovering how to compose effective and responsible e-mail messages.

WHEN WE COMMUNICATE THROUGH E-MAIL, WE PUT A LOT ON THE LINE

E-mail is everywhere! So many of us are connecting by sending and receiving e-mail every day. Many of us are online all the time, and we are communicating through e-mail more and more.

At work, we use e-mail to communicate with coworkers, team members, customers, and vendors. We send and receive memos, notes, letters, reports, and forms. All kinds of business correspondence happen through e-mail.

The shift from relying on snail mail, voice mail, or face-to-face communications to communicating mainly through e-mail has happened quickly. Most of us have not even slowed down long enough to realize what this form of communication is and does or how to use it best. We usually happen along, using e-mailing spontaneously, neither carefully composing our messages nor appearing composed through our electronic communications.

Then all of a sudden, we hear a horror story about employees being fired for misusing their e-mail or we experience the fallout from miscommunication firsthand. For a fleeting moment, we realize maybe we should pay attention to what we are saying and how we are appearing through e-mail. As quickly as we think these thoughts, though, we forget them. We never seem to have the luxury of time to think about our e-mail correspondence, let alone pay attention to what could be on the line there.

> *"When writing isn't as good as it could be, you and your organization pay a price in wasted time, wasted effort, and lost goodwill."*
>
> –Locker, 1995

Our Image

What about this image we create for ourselves through our e-mail? How do our e-mmunities *see* us through our messages? How do they *hear* us? How do they *feel* about us? How do they *respond* to us?

Even if the receivers of our e-mail know us in person, we may actually come across in e-mail communications with an entirely different persona. Think for a minute about your own e-mail history:

- Have your e-mail communications generally made you appear efficient, courteous, and organized?

- Might the receivers of your e-mail ever have thought of you as impulsive, rude, boorish, or even uncaring?

- Do you believe the members of your e-mmunities generally regard you as a brilliant collaborator?

- Might they ever see you as a stumbling, awkward communicator?

As a result of e-mail communications, our efficiency may even be challenged. When we are in the middle of a miscommunication, our reputation may suffer. If our writing is not tight enough, if we use too many extra words, or if our message is unclear or disorganized, we may actually gain the reputation of being inefficient.

If we send attachments no one can open, forget to supply enough context to an original message or reply, or supply too much information by forwarding all the messages in a long thread, we may appear lazy, inconsiderate, or unsavvy. We might even be thought of as uncooperative, and our team relationships may be threatened.

The Image of Our Organization

What further compounds the importance of our e-mail use on the job is that our communications represent not only who we are, but actually come to symbolize the organization we work for. So not only do we look good or not so good, we may actually be setting up other people in the organization for kudos or problems based on our e-mail communications. When we neglect to communicate responsibly and efficiently, we not only put our reputation on the line, we may also be putting other people's or our entire organization's reputation on the line.

> "... it would be unfortunate if your e-mail message did not produce the effect you had expected."
> –Whelen, 2000

If we use e-mail to communicate with customers, we must be especially mindful of the impressions we project. In addition to practicing good Netiquette, we must compose our e-mail messages carefully and deliberately. Otherwise, a customer may feel we do not care enough to take the time to write it right and may even equate a poor message with poor customer service.

Our E-mmunity Relationships

When we communicate with people regularly through e-mail, we form electronic communities or e-mmunities. Some e-mmunities explicitly outline communication rules or standards they want members to practice. These standards may even go beyond basic Netiquette guidelines. Sometimes, standards evolve over time, after a number of communications, or we may be left to our own perceptions to figure out what the rules are.

So how do we figure out what e-mail standards our e-mmunities require?

- They may tell us up front what the rules of communication are.
- They may make up the rules as the communications require.
- They may model preferred e-mail practices.
- They may send cues that our communications are okay or not okay.

Even if you already are confident you know how to write good memos, letters, and notes at work, e-mail's uniqueness requires specific kinds of considerations. *This chapter provides the basics you need to compose effective e-mails that fit accepted emerging e-mail standards and business writing conventions.*

GOOD WRITERS USE A PROCESS TO COMPOSE MESSAGES

Think about how you put together an e-mail message. How do you know where to begin? Do you just start writing, making up the message as you go along or do you follow some kind of composing process?

Each of us has some kind of process we use to **compose**, even if we are not fully aware of what that process is.

When we write, we consciously or unconsciously go through certain steps. By realizing what these steps are, we can take a closer look at our own writing process and then begin to improve it.

We may be using a writing process that has worked for us in the past when writing reports, memos, or letters on the job. Because e-mail is a unique form of business communication, we must make sure we have adapted our process to fit this task. We should also consider that our writing process may have originated in times when we mainly used paper and pens to write. When we compose e-mail, we word process and key our message directly on the computer in an e-mail program. Word processing with a computer enables us to easily revise and polish our messages.

> *"Whether it's a report , memo, or e-mail, good writing is essential to fast, effective communication."*
> –RaganWeb, 1998

> Definition of **process**: "a series of actions, changes, or functions bringing about a result."
> –American Heritage Dictionary of the English Language, 3rd ed., 1992

Reflection Activity	*Your Composing Process*

1. What do you do *before* you begin to write?

2. What do you do *while* you are writing?

3. What do you do *after* you write?

BEFORE WRITING

Before you begin to write, your composing process should include some steps for planning what your message will say.

1. Decide on the *purpose* for the message and the *action* you want as a result.

2. Collect the *information* you need for the message, keeping in mind who your *audience* is and what they will need to ensure that the message gets your intended results.

3. If you have any *attachments* to send, attach them now. If you wait until you are finished drafting and proofreading, you may forget.

4. Many users today are online or connected and ready to send as soon as they open their e-mail program. Some users have accidentally hit the send button before their message is complete. Be careful to review your message, recipient(s), or attachment(s), especially if you don't have to pause for an Internet connection.

5. You might *map* (on paper), *brainstorm, outline,* or *free write* (on the computer) the key elements of the message. Then you can compose your final message right on the screen using whatever you came up with during the planning.

We will now show you how to map, brainstorm, outline, and free write to create your message. We will provide an example of each then have you try it. We use the same topics for all methods so you can compare these different methods. When you prewrite your e-mails, you can then choose whichever method you are most comfortable with.

> *"An e-note should get to the point immediately— the way to do this is to plan what you intend to write."*
>
> —Stewart, 1999

> *"As a writer, you are in some ways like a bandleader. You must orchestrate all the elements of your writing into a persuasive performance, assembling your ideas, words, and evidence into one coherent structure. Readers expect you to be their guide—to help them understand your meaning."*
>
> —Lunsford and Connors, 1997

E-mail Map

One way to organize your thoughts before writing is to draw a map. A map helps you visually organize information for your e-mail. You begin by drawing a circle and writing the main topic inside. Then you draw lines moving out from the circle and write key elements to be communicated about the topic.

The following figure contains an example of an e-mail map to let managers know about an upcoming budget meeting.

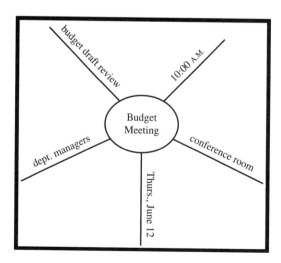

Practice Activity   *Map*

It is your turn to practice the mapping technique. Following are the beginnings of two maps.

Map 1—Cancel order: When a customer cancels an order that is already in the mail, what information might you, as the vendor, include in a return e-mail? Write each piece of information on a line coming out from the middle circle. Add lines if you would include more information.*

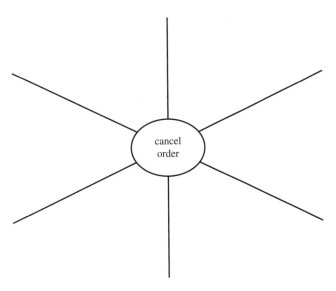

Map 2—Office party: What information might you include in an e-mail invitation to an office party? Write each piece of information on a line coming out from the middle circle. Add lines if you would include more information.

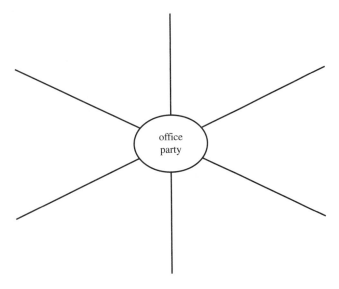

*Turn to page 156 for our suggested map for canceling an order.

E-mail Brainstorm

Another way to organize your thoughts before writing is to brainstorm ideas. You select your main topic and list key elements to be communicated about the topic. You can brainstorm using your e-mail software so you do not have to key the information again.

The following figure contains an example of an e-mail brainstorm for the same budget meeting discussed in the e-mail example.

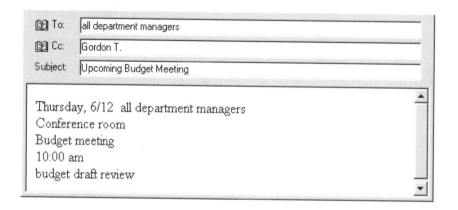

Practice Activity   *Brainstorm*

It is your turn to practice the brainstorming technique. Following are the same two examples we used in our mapping practice.

Brainstorm 1—Cancel order: Brainstorm a list of information in answer to the question, "When a customer cancels an order that is already in the mail, what information might you need to put in a return e-mail?"*

Cancel order:

Brainstorm 2—Office party: Brainstorm the information you might include in an e-mail invitation to an office party. Create a list of bulleted items to be included.

Office party:

*Turn to page 157 for our suggested brainstorm for canceling an order.

> "Shape your e-mail message so that it has a structure that is easy to follow. This is crucial to communicating your points quickly. Not addressing your reader, randomly presenting topics, or disregarding structural enhancements are all factors that slow down the reader trying to make sense of your message."
>
> −Angell and Heslop, 1998

E-mail Outline

A third way to organize your thoughts before writing is to use an outline. You select your main topic and outline key elements to be communicated about the topic.

The following figure contains an example of an e-mail outline of who, what, where, when, why, and how for the same budget meeting.

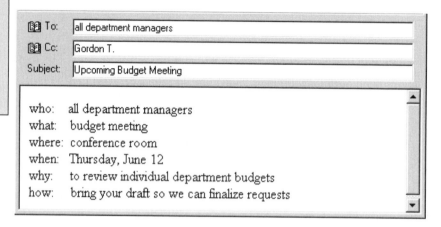

Practice Activity   *Outline*

It is your turn to practice the outlining technique. Following are the same two examples we used in our mapping and brainstorming practices.

Outline 1—Cancel order: Create an outline of key information, using the 5 W's and H: who, what, where, when, why, and how.*

Cancel order

who:

what:

where:

when:

why:

how:

Outline 2—Office party: Outline the information you might include in an e-mail invitation to an office party. Identify the who, what, where, when, and how to be included.

Office party:

who:

what:

where:

when:

why:

how:

*Turn to page 157 for our suggested outline for canceling an order.

E-mail Free Write

A fourth way to organize your thoughts before writing is to free write. You select your main topic and write your thoughts about what must be communicated about the topic.

The following figure contains an example of an e-mail free write for the same budget meeting.

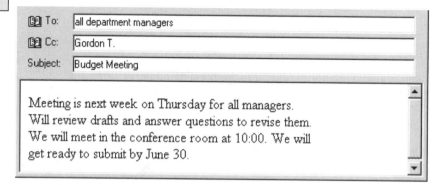

To: all department managers
Cc: Gordon T.
Subject: Budget Meeting

Meeting is next week on Thursday for all managers.
Will review drafts and answer questions to revise them.
We will meet in the conference room at 10:00. We will
get ready to submit by June 30.

Practice Activity — *Free Write*

It is your turn to practice the free writing technique. Following are the same two topics we used in our mapping, brainstorming, and outlining practices.

Free Write 1—Cancel order: Write your thoughts on the key points you would need to make in a return e-mail to a customer who cancels an order that is already in the mail.*

Free Write 2—Office party: Free write the information you might include in an e-mail invitation to an office party.

*Turn to page 157 for our suggested outline for canceling an order.

E-mail Final Copy

After using a map, brainstorm, outline, or free write, you can **draft** your e-mail and then compose your final version.

The following figure contains an example of an e-mail final copy.

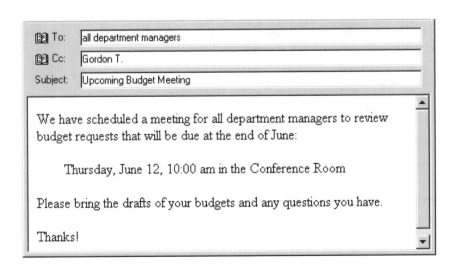

To: all department managers
Cc: Gordon T.
Subject: Upcoming Budget Meeting

We have scheduled a meeting for all department managers to review budget requests that will be due at the end of June:

Thursday, June 12, 10:00 am in the Conference Room

Please bring the drafts of your budgets and any questions you have.

Thanks!

DURING WRITING

As you begin to write or draft from your plan, your composing process should include the next set of steps.

1. As you draft, think of how the *words you choose* represent you and create an *image* of you to the recipients of your e-mail messages.

2. You also should think about how you will *organize* and *display* your message to be the most effective in this communication.

3. "Sell" your message using the *subject line.* Your recipient(s) will decide what to do with your message based on what they see in the e-mail header—especially the subject line.

Fill in the *subject line* after you have drafted your message to make sure you:

■ Summarize the essence of your message in as few words as possible.

■ Capture the receiver's attention so the message will be read.

■ Do not use "FYI" in the subject line because people get FYI's all the time and may actually delete these messages without even bothering to open them.

■ Realize the recipient may file your message and have to use the subject line to retrieve the message in the future.

> *"Those of us who wish to succeed need to become better with words. We need to be able to write better so that our words have more of a chance to rise above the massive traffic jam of words that the world has become."*
>
> –McGovern, 2001

> *"Prefer a specific subject line that informs to one that merely suggests a topic."*
>
> –Booher, 2001

> *Do use subject headers in all of your e-mails so that the recipient can quickly reference your in-coming e-mail and know what it is about.*
>
> –Chase and Trupp, 2000

Sample Subject Lines

Poor—the subject line is not used to show the stage of the e-mail conversation.

Original Message

    Subject: Customer Complaint

First Reply

    Subject: Customer Complaint

Second Reply

    Subject: Customer Complaint

Better—the subject line is used to show the stage of the e-mail conversation

Original Message

    Subject: Resolved Billing for Acme Widget – 7/19/01

First Reply

    Subject: Follow-up Actions to Resolved Billing for Acme Widget – 7/19/01

Second Reply

    Subject: Reply from Acme Widget after Resolved

Reflection Activity   *Subject Lines*

Over the next few days, pay attention to the subject lines on the e-mails you receive. Which ones are effective? Why? Which ones could be better? How would you improve them?

AFTER WRITING

Once your message is keyed in, you should take the time to review what you have said. Remember responsible e-mail users work with an e-mail buddy inside or outside the e-mmunity to help them compose messages and give feedback. Here is your opportunity to make sure you and your e-mail Buddy proofread to check your message for:

- **Spelling** — *Use your spell check* if it is part of your e-mail word processing program. You could also check your spelling carefully or have someone else proofread your message.

- **Punctuation** — Even though e-mail sometimes is a bit more "chatty" than other forms of business communication, you still must use punctuation to *help the reader navigate through the message.* Punctuation serves a purpose and *helps make the meaning of your message clear.* Also be sure not to overuse punctuation, even when you want to make a point.

- **Grammar and usage** — Take the time to make sure your e-mail message is grammatically correct and that it makes sense. *Use your grammar check,* if you have one, and *read your message out loud.* You'd be surprised how easily you can catch errors using this straightforward, simple check of your own words.

- **Accuracy** — Make sure you have included all the correct *names, dates, numbers, e-mail addresses, and other details.* You will cause a lot of confusion if you send incorrect or incomplete information to a customer, vendor, or coworker.

- **Organization** — *Check to see that your purpose is clearly stated* up front and that your *question* or required *action* is the last part of your message. Make sure that the way you have laid out the details makes sense and that your *message flows* in a logical way and is easy to follow.

- **Formatting** — Make sure you have used enough *paragraphing, spacing,* and *bulleting* to allow important details to stand out. Be careful not to bury information in a blob of text. Use *lists, headings, and subheadings.* Remember, most readers will just skim their e-mail, so make your message easy for them to skim.

    Be careful not to use bullets, bolding, italics, underlining, or automatic numbering unless you are sure the receiver's e-mail software can interpret special formatting. Use an asterisk (*) or hyphen (-) as a bullet. Use keystrokes such as asterisks (*) to signal items in a list, titles, or anything else you want to stand out. For example, replace the italics in a title with asterisks—*Gone with the Wind.*

    Sample formatting of e-mail message

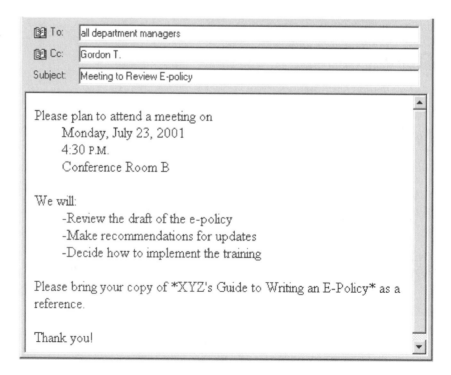

A GOOD E-MAIL MESSAGE FOLLOWS THE 10 C'S

E-mail should be:

- **Clear** so that the purpose of the message is not hidden or buried.

- **Concise** and collapsed and does not use extra words or business-speak.

- **Correct** and contains accurate names, dates, and details.

- **Conscious** of the recipient's needs and mindful of the image projected.

- **Complete** enough not to require a follow-up communication because something was left out.

- **Considerate** and shows thought for the person on the other side of the communication.

- **Courteous**, uses a polite tone, and is an example of excellent Netiquette.

- **Consistent** about how information is represented, how people are addressed, and how salutations and closings are expressed.

- **Concrete** and firmly and openly states the required action.

- **Connecting** to strengthen relationships and build goodwill.

> *"By sending clear and informative e-mail messages, you can avoid sending and receiving repeat e-mails."*
> –Red Earth Software, 2001

> *"Writing clearly means getting your message across without the person on the receiving end having to work hard to understand it."*
> –Whelan, 2000

GOOD WRITERS ARE ALWAYS AWARE OF THEIR AUDIENCES

Your primary **audience** in an e-mail communication is the person to whom the message is addressed. The secondary audience is made up of anyone to whom the message is copied. Because e-mail is *never* private, anyone may be privy to the contents of the e-mail.

Remember, e-mail can be forwarded to anyone who has an e-mail address. Even if people do not have computers or do not communicate through e-mail, they can wind up with paper copies of e-mail messages. *We never know where our e-mail messages will land.*

When considering your audiences you should anticipate:

- *Whom* should the message be addressed to?

- *Who* should be cc'd (copied)?

- *Whom* might the message be forwarded to?

- *What* do recipients already know about the topic or discussion?

- How much *context* should you provide?

> *"A piece of writing requires at least two people: one to write it and one to read it. Who's going to read yours? It's important to ask, because people who don't know their readers or who forget about them aren't very good writers. You'll save yourself all kinds of trouble by learning this lesson early."*
> –O'Connor, 1999

- What *impressions* does this audience already have about you or the topic?

- What *barriers* might you foresee to getting the required action?

- What kind of *reply* or *actions* do you expect?

- What are their *expectations* for your e-mail messages regarding the level of formality?

GOOD WRITERS ALSO PAY ATTENTION TO THE CRITICAL ATTRIBUTES OF THEIR MESSAGES

Because e-mail has replaced the office memo and is also replacing letters and notes, we must consider everything we did in traditional business writing *and more*:

Tone

Business communications should always have a professional, positive tone even if the message contains some bad news. Make sure you:

- Use positive words and avoid negative words.

- Avoid sarcasm or any words that can be misinterpreted.

- Use a buffer to introduce any news that may be considered controversial. See the following figure for an example. (Remember, if the information is sensitive, confidential, or negative, you should not send it via e-mail. You should probably schedule a face-to-face meeting to convey the news.)

> *Definition of* **buffer**: "A neutral or positive statement designed to allow the writer to bury, or buffer, the negative message."*
>
> –Locker, 1995

```
┌──────────────────────────────────────────────────────────────┐
│  📖 To:     │John E.                                           │
│  📖 Cc:     │                                                  │
│  Subject:   │Your widget delivery                              │
├──────────────────────────────────────────────────────────────┤
│                                                                │
│  John:                                                         │
│                                                                │
│  I enjoyed meeting with you yesterday to discuss your order    │
│  of 300 widgets from our company. You are always pleasant to   │
│  work with!                                                    │
│                                                                │
│  The order will actually arrive at your plant on May 10        │
│  instead of May 3, as originally planned. We had a change in   │
│  our production schedule, and we will need at least the extra  │
│  week.                                                         │
│                                                                │
│  Please contact me if you prefer to receive the order after    │
│  May 10.                                                       │
│                                                                │
│  Thank you!                                                    │
│  -Rod                                                          │
│                                                                │
└──────────────────────────────────────────────────────────────┘
```

Reflection Activity	*Subject Tone*

Have you ever received an e-mail with a harsh tone? Have you ever sent one that was misinterpreted?

Context

When you originate an e-mail communication, you must make sure you give the recipient enough background information to read the message without much effort or thought.

When you reply to an e-mail, you have to be sure you supply enough context so recipients remember what conversation they are in. Remember, as people get more and more e-mail, they may need a bit more prompting with each conversation so they do not get lost.

- Supply enough information in the initial message so the recipient does not have to perform additional activities to complete the requested action.

- In a threaded conversation, reply by including the entire original message, a selection of the message, or a summary of the message. Be careful not to commit overkill and include too much information.

Readability

E-mail is supposed to be quick, efficient, and convenient. Recipients of e-mail expect to be able to read their e-mail messages and take the required action. One way to help the communication go smoothly is to pay attention to the attributes of a message that make it readable. You should do the following to help your readers:

- Use a large enough font size: 12 to 14 points is a good standard.

- Use paragraphs and skip a line between paragraphs to help the reader skim through the message.

- Stay on purpose, covering only one or two short topics per message.

> *"The opportunity is that there is so much information; the catastrophe is that 99 percent of it isn't meaningful or understandable."*
> —Wurman, 2001

> *"Have you ever received a message that attempts to fulfill many different purposes at once? The result is often confusion and a train of subsequent messages."*
> —Whelan, 2000

- Write in a formal businesslike, professional style by using short, familiar words and short sentences. Avoid using outdated "**business-speak**," stuffy expressions, or jargon.

- Pay attention to how you format your message. Use white space and list or bullet details so they are easy to pick out.

- End with the question you want answered or the action you need accomplished as a result of the message.

- Keep your message short enough to fit on one screen. Avoid making the reader scroll the message.

Verbs

Use verbs to carry the meaning of your message, because e-mails should primarily be written to further action.

- Use present tense as much as possible to relate to the here and now.

- Use active voice (bottom figure), which is shorter and easier to understand than passive voice (top figure), and helps us further action.

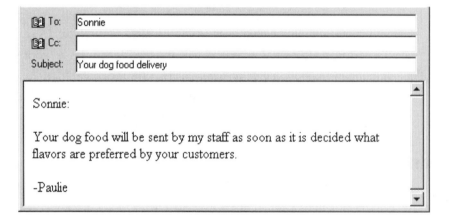

TOOLS & TIPS

Hot Tools & Tips!

The remaining pages in this chapter contain a quiz and job guides such as tips, checklists, and references.

✓   **QUICK CHECK***

1. You should wait until you are done drafting your e-mail before adding attachments, in case you change your mind about what to send.   True or False?

2. Two ways to plan what you are going to write include:

3. An effective subject line should:

4. When composing an e-mail, you should make sure you have used paragraphs and spacing to allow important details to stand out.   True or False?

5. Proofreading includes verifying names, dates, numbers, e-mail addresses, phone numbers, and other details.   True or False?

6. List three of the 10 C's of good communication:

7. When thinking about your audience for an e-mail message, you really do not have to worry about what kind of reply to expect.   True or False?

8. Define secondary audience.

9. When should you use a buffer?

10. Using a 10-point font is usually a good standard for e-mail.   True or False?

*Turn to page 154 for answers to the Quick Check.

WOW (Words of Wisdom)

Composing E-mail at Work

1. Remember to pay attention to your writing process and take care to plan, consciously write, and review your e-mail before sending it off.

2. Remember the 10 C's of writing e-mail: be clear, concise, correct, conscious, complete, considerate, courteous, consistent, concrete, and connected.

3. Always be aware of your audiences and be sure to anticipate the best ways to communicate to them.

4. Pay attention to the critical attributes of your message: tone, context, readability, and verbs.

5. Take care to write a clear, meaningful subject line to summarize the meaning of your message and to catch the reader's attention.

6. Avoid using "business-speak," stuffy expressions, and jargon.

7. Remember most of all, your e-mails reflect your image and the image of your organization, so always put your best foot forward.

Tiptionary	*More Questions I Should Ask Myself Before Dashing Off E-mail*

- ☐ Am I satisfied that I projected a good image of myself and my organization through this e-mail?

- ☐ Have I been mindful of my audience and how my message will be received?

- ☐ Have I checked to see that all my information, including dates, names, and e-mail addresses, is accurate?

- ☐ Have I included any attachments I want to send?

- ☐ Was I careful to check my message especially if my e-mail program is always connected to the Internet?

- ☐ Is my tone professional and businesslike?

- ☐ Does my subject line capture the essence of my message and will it capture the attention of the recipient?

- ☐ Are my spelling and grammar correct?

- ☐ Have I used paragraphs and enough white space to help my recipients easily skim my message and understand how they need to respond?

- ☐ Am I supplying enough background information or context so my recipients will know what action is required and whom the message is from?

- ☐ Have I written in simple, short sentences and used clear, simple words?

- ☐ Am I confident the recipient will easily know what to do with my message?

| Tiptionary | *Composing Effective E-mail Messages* |

Before writing, always make sure to:

- ☐ Decide on the purpose for the message and the action you want as a result.
- ☐ Collect information.
- ☐ Analyze your audience.
- ☐ Add attachments.
- ☐ Map, brainstorm, or free write.

↓

During writing, be careful to:

- ☐ Choose the right words.
- ☐ Remember the image you want to create.
- ☐ Think about how to organize the information to maximize the intended results.
- ☐ Decide how you will display the message.
- ☐ Consciously fill in the subject line.

↓

After writing, proofread to:

- ☐ Check spelling, punctuation, and grammar.
- ☐ Verify names, dates, numbers, e-mail addresses, and other details.
- ☐ Make sure you have organized the message correctly.
- ☐ Make sure you have formatted your message to make the message easy for the recipient to read.
- ☐ Use your Tiptionaries.
- ☐ Use your e-mail Style Guide in the appendix.
- ☐ Have an e-mail buddy edit for tone, readability, and completeness.

Tiptionary	*Tone: Negative Words to Avoid*	
afraid	hesitate	objection
anxious	ignorant	problem
avoid	ignore	reject
bad	impossible	sorry
careless	in- words:	terrible
damage	inadequate	trivial
delay	incomplete	trouble
delinquent	inconvenient	un- words:
deny	insincere	unclear
difficulty	injury	unfair
dis- words:	lacking	unfortunate
disapprove	loss	unpleasant
dishonest	mis- words:	unreasonable
dissatisfied	misfortune	unreliable
eliminate	mistake	unsure
error	missing	wait
except	neglect	weakness
fail	never	worry
fault	no	wrong
fear	not	

Tiptionary | *Words Often Misspelled*

After you write, proofread to check spelling . . .

a lot	believe	every day
accept	business	exercise
against	cannot	experience
all right	categories	finally
apparent	definitely	immediate
argument	dependent	may be
before	develop	necessary
beginning	environment	noticeable
occasion	separate	where
occurred	success	whether
occurrences	successful	without
professor	through	woman
received	truly	
sense	until	

Tiptionary — *Words Often Confused*

While you write, be careful to choose the right word . . .

accept—to take or receive
except—with the exclusion of

affect—to have an influence; accomplish
effect—result; to cause to happen

amount—use with concepts that cannot be counted individually but can be measured
number—use when items can be counted individually

are—form of "be"
our—belonging to us

between—use with only two choices
among—use with more than two choices

cite—to refer to
sight—seeing, something seen
site—location

complement—something that completes
compliment—praise

conscience—sense of right and wrong
conscious—mentally aware

fewer—use for objects that can be counted individually
less—use for objects that can be measured but not counted individually

forth—forward
fourth—4th

its—belonging to it
it's—it is; it has

lie—to recline; to tell a falsehood
lay—to put an object on something

loose—not tight
lose—to misplace; to fail to win

principal—most important; head of a school
principle—fundamental truth

respectfully—with respect
respectively—to each in the order listed

sense—feeling, intelligence
since—from the time that

than—as compared with
then—at that time; therefore

their—belonging to them
there—in that place
they're—they are

threw—past tense of throw
thorough—complete
through—in one side of and out the other; by means of

to—in the direction of
too—also, excessive
two—2

who's—who is; who has
whose—belonging to whom

your—belonging to you
you're—you are

Tiptionary	*Some Business-Speak to Avoid*
Stuffy Expression	**Crisp Expression**
at this point in time	now
at a later date	later
due to the fact that	because
for the purpose that	because
in the event that	if
in the neighborhood of	about
on a monthly basis	monthly
make an inquiry regarding	ask about
without further delay	now
do not hesitate to call me	call me
enclosed please find	I have enclosed or I have attached

Tiptionary	*Quick Capitalization and Sentence Structure Review*

Always capitalize:

1. **the first word of a sentence**

2. **proper nouns** (We shipped your order to the following address: 101 Elm Street, Columbus, Ohio.)

3. **titles before proper names** (Ms. Smith, Dr. Jones, Professor Reed)

4. **titles of works: books, CDs, art, videos** (book - *Business Netiquette,* CD – *The Jimi Hendrix Experience,* painting – *The Mona Lisa,* video – *Shine*)
   (Remember: When writing in e-mail, you must also use asterisks to set off a title, replacing the italics or underlining you would otherwise use.)

5. **names of specific products** (Razor Scooter, Madeline's Dollhouse, Idealist Skin Refresher)

6. **brand or trade names** (Estee Lauder, Michelin)

Always write a complete sentence:

1. **Include a *subject*** (The *shoes* are purple and blue.)

2. **Include a *verb*** (The chalk *scratched* the blackboard.)

Use this structure as a guideline for a simple, straightforward, and easy to read sentence:

1. **subject** (We)

2. **verb** (shipped)

3. **object** (the order)

4. **adverb** (today)

We shipped the order today.

Tiptionary	*Quick Punctuation Review*

Use an **apostrophe:**

1. In a contraction to indicate that one or more letters have been omitted. (We'll meet at 3:00 P.M. today.)

2. To indicate possession, including when one noun in a comparison is omitted. (This year's sale will be higher than last year's.)

3. To make plurals that could be confused for other words. (I earned A's in my business writing classes.)

Use a **colon:**

1. To show that a list follows a main clause. (Please order the following supplies: pens, pads, and copy paper.)

2. To follow the salutation in a business letter or e-mail. (Dear Ms. Jones:)

Use a **comma:**

1. To separate words that interrupt the sentence. (Nancy, could you please send me a copy of your resume? I interviewed Nancy, Ron's assistant, for the new position.)

2. After the first clause in a compound sentence if the clauses are long or if they each have a subject. (I had asked her to bring her resume to the meeting, and she forgot it the first time.)

3. To separate items in a series. (Please order the following supplies: pens, pads, and copy paper.)

Use a **hyphen:**

1. To join two or more words used as a single adjective. (Please conduct the follow-up study soon.)

Use a **semicolon:**

1. To join two closely related independent clauses. (We'll do our best to fill your order promptly; however, we cannot guarantee a delivery date.)

2. To separate items in a series when the items themselves contain commas. (The final choices for the new plant are El Paso, Texas; Columbus, Ohio; and Boulder, Colorado.)

Key Terms

Audience   Context

Business-speak   Draft

Compose   Formatting

References

Angell, D. and Heslop, B. (1994). *The elements of e-mail style*. Reading, PA: Addison-Wesley Publishing Company.

Booher, D. (2001). *E-Writing*. New York: Pocket Books.

Chase, M. and Trupp, S. (2000). *Office e-mails that really click*. Newport: Aegis Publishing Group, Ltd.

Covey, S. R. (1989). *The 7 habits of highly effective people*. New York: Fireside.

Lamb, L. and Peek, J. (1995). *Using e-mail effectively*. Sebastopol, CA: O'Reilly & Associates, Inc.

Locker, K. O. (1995). *Business and administrative communication*, 3rd ed. Chicago: Irwin.

Lunsford, A. and Connors, C. (1997). *The everyday writer*. New York: St. Martin's Press, Inc.

McGovern, G. (2001, July 5). The text revolution. *ClickZ*. Available: www.clickz.com/article/cz.4077.html [2001, July 5].

O'Conner, P. T. (1999). *Words fail me*. New York: Harcourt Brace & Co.

Red Earth Software (2001). How to send effective e-mail replies. www.redearthsoftware.com/Download.htm [2001, July 16]

Stewart, J. (1999, November 30). E-mail: what's in and what's out. *InternetDay*. Available: www.internetday.com/archives/113099-text.html [1999, November 30].

Trelease, F. J. (1999, November 18). Nobody answers your business e-mail? *USA Today*. Available: www.usatoday.womenconnect.com.../nov1899_biz.htm?LAFCodeOverride=USA TODA [1999, December 2].

Whelan, J. (2000). *E-mail @ work*. Edinburgh Gate: Pearson Education Limited.

Whelen, J. (2000). *E-mail@work: Get moving with digital communication*. London: ft.com

Wurman, R. S. (2001). *Information anxiety 2*. Indianapolis, Indiana: Que.

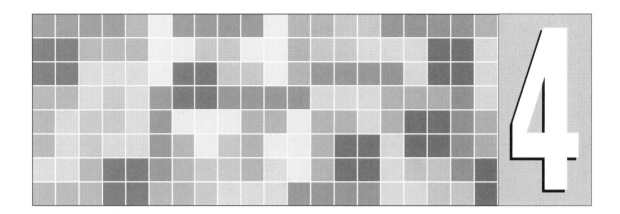

Managing the Barrage of E-mail: Using a System to Organize, Process, and Declutter

"Besides the noble art of getting things done, there is the noble art of leaving things undone. The wisdom of life lies in eliminating the nonessentials."

Chinese Proverb

WHAT YOU'LL LEARN IN THIS CHAPTER

Goal

- To provide simple strategies for managing your e-mail

Objectives

As a result of this training, you should be able to:

- Organize your files into working files, reference files, and archive files

- ■ Process using the:
    - ☐ 4 R's: Read to Do, Respond, Review, Revisit
    - ☐ 4 S's: Scan, Skim, Study, and Sort
    - ☐ 5 D's: Delete, Delegate, Do Now, Delay, and Dock
    - ☐ 2 F's: Follow through and Follow up
- ■ Declutter by keeping your own and your e-mmunities' (electronic communities' or organization's) mailboxes tidy

---

ASSESS YOUR E-MAIL MANAGEMENT QUOTIENT (EQ)

Check ☑ the following statements that describe your management of e-mail.

☐ 1. Do you ever feel bombarded with unnecessary, poorly written, or just plain junk e-mail?

☐ 2. Are you not keeping your mailbox tidy, causing your organization's e-mail database to grow out of control?

☐ 3. Do you presently have more than 10 e-mails in your in box?

☐ 4. Do you presently have more than 10 e-mails in your sent items box?

☐ 5. Do you save copies of e-mails in your mailbox to remind you to make appointments or contacts or to schedule actions?

☐ 6. Do you ever respond to "jam" (unsolicited jokes, chain letters, or inspirational messages from friends) because you are afraid to have bad luck or disappoint someone?

☐ 7. Do you spend more than 1 hour a day doing e-mail chores?

☐ 8. Do you ever take more than a few days to respond to your incoming e-mails?

☐ 9. Do you ever feel like e-mail is the curse of the millennium?

☐ 10. Does your e-mail box resemble electronic "piles" rather than electronic files?

If you placed a check next to three or more of these questions, you probably need to develop a system for managing the barrage of e-mail. Then you can use your electronic communications to get the results you and your electronic community intend.

Here begins your adventure of "staying on purpose" and "keeping the order."

WE HAVE GONE FROM "YOU'VE GOT MAIL!" TO "OH NO! NOW WHAT?!"

"The Electronic Messaging Association estimates this year 108 million e-mail users will receive over 7 trillion e-mail messages—about 65,000 each if you're counting...."

—Wurman, 2001

"We've all become pro-sumers: consumers and producers of content."

—Wurman, 2001

"International Data Corporation (IDC) has predicted that 35 billion e-mails will be sent every day by 2005."

—IDC Research reported in Nua Internet Surveys, 2000

It was a thrill! We were enamored of our first "You've got mail!" What a wonderful thing—to be connected so quickly and intimately with so many people. We could connect with other people day and night, for so many purposes, to say just about anything we felt moved to express. E-mail was a blessing.

Or was it? Somehow that trickle of heralded e-mails with its accompanying thrill turned into "raging torrents of consciousness" bombarding us and rubbing our already raw nerves. Has the once beloved blessing now become a dreaded curse? Is our honeymoon with e-mail over?

Because we will be living with e-mail for a long, long time, we probably should figure out how to keep the romance alive. True, we often feel we are repeatedly buried in a barrage of e-mail, but somewhere in that heap are the gems we seek. Making our way through the heap to find the gems is the trick. Sorting through the office banter, the FYIs, and the unsolicited jokes, jam, and junk to find the gems is the challenge.

What we need is a system for organizing, processing, and decluttering our e-mmunities' (electronic communities') collective electronic conversations. *This chapter presents strategies and solutions to help us manage the barrage of e-mail*—not only for ourselves, but for our entire e-mmunity. The time has come to "clean up the neighborhood."

THE BARRAGE OF INFORMATION CAN BE A DRAIN ON PRODUCTIVITY

"Killer app that it is, e-mail is also a serious productivity drain. The typical U.S. worker receives over 200 e-mails per day, according to a new Pitney Bowes survey. That's a staggering 1,000 messages a week to deal with—read, reply, delete and/or ignore."

—Berst, 1999

In addition to e-mail, workers are barraged with information from many other sources. No wonder we all feel trapped and stressed by information overload. We need effective time and information management strategies and practices so we can be more productive.

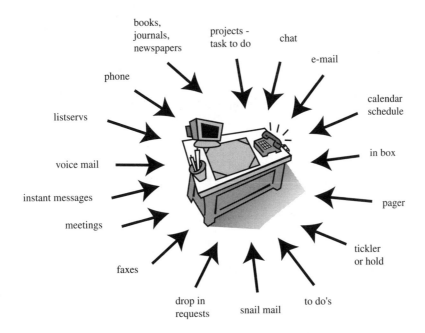

Where did the day go? In addition to face-to-face meetings, we must master managing over 200 messages per day on average. The number and type of messages we send and receive look something like this:

> *"Time wasted on personal e-mail and spam . . . resulted in a loss of 115 hours of productivity per employee [per year] . . . "*
> –Ferris Research reported in Nua Internet Surveys, 2000

Number and Types of Messages per Day

Type of Message	Number
Phone	52
E-mail	36
Voice mail	23
Postal mail	18
Interoffice mail	18
Fax	14
Post-it notes	13
Telephone slips	9
Pager	8
Cell phone	4
Overnight courier service	4
U.S. Postal Service express mail	3

Source: Pitney Bowes Inc. in Crowley, 1999

If we were to add up the time we spend reading, writing, and acting on our e-mail alone, we would be astonished. Plus, *the number of e-mails we send and receive each day is growing*. In many organizations, e-mail has actually become the *preferred form of business communication*. For some people, e-mail is quickly growing out of control. What will happen to us if we do not get a handle on this monster now?

Reflection Activity — *Where Does Your Day Go?*

Keep a record of the time you spend on your business communications. Record the amount of time you spend on messages you receive and send in a typical work week. If you deal with message types not already listed, add them to the bottom of the list. At the end of 5 days, calculate the average time spent for each type of message.

Time Spent

Type of Message	Day 1	Day 2	Day 3	Day 4	Day 5	Average
Phone						
E-mail						
Chat or instant messages						
Voice mail						
Postal mail						
Interoffice mail						
Fax						
Post-it or handwritten notes						
Telephone slips						
Pager						
Cell phone						
Overnight courier service						
Express mail						

Reflection Activity	*Saving Time—Your Most Precious Resource*

Processing your business communications more efficiently and effectively could save you from 15 minutes to 2 hours a day. How much time would you like to save?

Fill out the following table to calculate the value of time you could save on the job.

	Sample Savings	**Your Savings**
1. Hourly wage	$25	
2. Hours per working day	8	
3. Total average daily wage (1 × 2)	$200	
4. Working days per year	230	
5. Total average yearly wage (3 × 4)	$46,000	
6. 15 minute savings in a 480-minute work day	.0312	
7. Yearly savings of 15 minutes a day (5 × 6)	$1,435.20	

E-MAIL SHOULD INCREASE EFFICIENCY AND EFFECTIVENESS

Communicating through e-mail can add to the *productivity drain* rather than the *productivity gain* when we take part in some bad, or even ugly, e-mail practices:

- Office banter and "flame wars" (nasty notes sent back and forth) take time and energy to participate in and often serve no purpose other than to waste time and cause frustration.

- Spam (unsolicited e-mail from solicitors) is generally a nuisance. Jam (unsolicited e-mail from friends) usually seduces us to read it and maybe even respond.

- Poorly written e-mail can result in miscommunications that take additional communications to straighten out.

- Improperly distributed e-mail—to the wrong recipients or to unnecessary recipients—can cause us to be distracted and confused.

- Viruses, carried through improperly handled e-mails, can infest your system and cause a series of problems—from computers crashing to whole systems becoming immobilized.

- Too many e-mails stored in our mailboxes cause systems to overload and make us work too hard to retrieve a message. We may cause a *paperless pile* to accumulate that can be messier than a paper pile to straighten out.

Of course we have more in our job descriptions than "communicate with others." So where do we find time to do anything else? How do we make the most of this mission critical communication channel? How and where do we begin to manage our e-mail communications so that they help us get the results we intend?

Reflection Activity   *Your Productivity Drains*

Look at the list of poor e-mail practices previously listed. Which ones have caused you trouble?

KEEP THE E-MMUNITY IN MIND BY ATTENDING TO *PURPOSE, POLICY*, AND *PROTOCOL*

As a basis for effective and responsible electronic communications, we must understand that when we communicate at work, we do so for specific reasons and with certain formalities and boundaries. Otherwise, our communications would be a free-for-all. Communication and information systems exist to support the larger systems of the organization and the work communities we belong to.

*Definition of **purpose**: "1. The object toward which one strives or for which something exists; goal; aim. 2. A result or effect that is intended or desired; intention."*

–The American Heritage Dictionary of the English Language, 1992

David Whyte (1994) discusses the purpose of a corporation: "to achieve things that would be impossible alone." He points out the root of the word, "corpus," refers to a body or part of a living organism that functions for one purpose. In our organizations, we work together as a unified group to fulfill a specific purpose. Whyte also reminds us that our collective purpose cannot be achieved by individuals working alone. So if e-mail communication is the preferred channel that connects us to other people at work, shouldn't we communicate with our business needs always in mind?

To communicate effectively and responsibly, each communication must align with the organization's purpose, policy, and protocol.

Reflection Activity   *What's My Purpose?*

1. What was I hired to accomplish?

2. How does this contribute to my department's or team's purpose?

3. How does this contribute to the organization's purpose?

4. How can I make sure I am aware of the purpose in every communication?

Purpose—*why the organization or team exists.* As Covey (1989) states, "begin with the end in mind." Business communications must focus on actions that further the collective purpose and align with the mission and goals of the business.

Policy—what the organization, electronic community, or team has articulated as *acceptable behaviors at work.* Policies are set to help a diverse group of human beings come to an agreement about how best to communicate to fulfill the group's collective purpose. Business communications must be conducted according to the guidelines set in written policies so that everyone puts forth a unified purpose and image.

> *Definition of* **policy:** *"1. Any plan or course of action adopted by a government, political party, business organization, or the like, designed to influence and determine decisions, actions, and other matters."*
>
> —*The American Heritage Dictionary of the English Language, 1992*

Reflection Activity   *What's Our Policy?*

1. Does my organization have a policy?

2. When was the last time I saw it?

3. Do I remember what it outlines?

4. How can I get a copy?

5. Whom do I contact to get a copy of the policy or create one if one does not exist?

Protocol—*unwritten rules of acceptable behavior at work* not explicitly articulated by the organization. In our electronic communications at work, our e-mmunities silently dictate rules by practicing certain behaviors. These behaviors are based on protocols that have become part of the organization's culture. These protocols guide us in communicating in consistent and reliable ways and eventually will become conventions of writing e-mail for everyone. An organization's protocols might influence such e-mail practices as:

> *Definition of* **protocol:** *"A code prescribing strict adherence to correct etiquette and precedence."*
>
> —*The Language Center, 2001*

- how quickly you respond to messages
- what rules of Netiquette (Internet etiquette) you emphasize

- how long your messages are

- what kinds of attachments you send

- how you deal with your e-mail when you are away on vacation or traveling for business

Until more conventions are agreed upon, set, and explicitly stated, we must be perceptive and proactive to consciously and intentionally figure out what to do and what not to do when using e-mail to communicate.

Reflection Activity   *Your E-mmunity's Protocols*

What are the protocols, or agreed upon e-mail behaviors already in place in your e-mmunities? Do your customers, vendors, coworkers, and friends have different standards of behavior? What are the behaviors, either stated or implied? If protocol has not been established, what behaviors should you establish?

E-mmunity	What is the protocol?	What should the protocol be?
Customers		
Vendors		
Coworkers		
Friends		
Others?		

MANAGING THE BARRAGE OF E-MAIL REQUIRES USING A SYSTEM

Just as you organize your file cabinet with your paper folders and files, you should manage your e-mails. Remember, you can accumulate *piles of papers* on your desk and in you office, and you can accumulate *piles of electronic data* on your computer and network.

If you never filed your papers systematically, you would have so much clutter, disorganization, and disarray you might create physical hazards and feel trapped, disoriented, and overwhelmed. Your electronic data can create barriers and cause you to feel the same horrible feelings if you do not include your e-mail messages as a part of your overall time and information management strategies.

With a system in place, you can better manage and handle organizing, processing, and decluttering your e-mail messages. Then you can keep your e-mmunities' collective electronic conversations healthy and moving freely. You can move from information to action to results more efficiently. You can begin to work smarter, not harder.

Cleaning up the neighborhood takes some effort, commitment, and intention. But the effort pays off and work-related habits can be successfully changed in 3 days to 3 weeks with consistent practice and persistence. You will see the results if you use a system.

An e-mail management system centers on these three main functions:

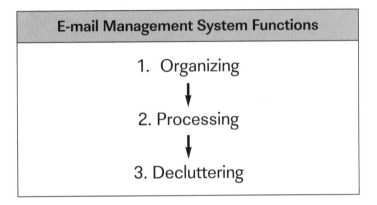

1. Organizing

The first function in setting up an e-mail management system is organizing. Organizing e-mail involves creating file categories, then setting routines and making these routines into habits.

The purpose of organizing is to help you retrieve information quickly and easily once you have moved your e-mail messages from your mailbox.

Organizing requires an initial setup then requires a watchful eye for continuous improvement.

2. Processing

The next function in an e-mail management system is processing, which involves reading to determine actions, prioritizing, scheduling, doing, and following up.

The purpose of processing is to help you move quickly through your pile of e-mails to get down to the business of business. Efficient processing helps you determine what tasks should be done or scheduled by whom, for whom, and in what order.

Processing is an ongoing function and depends on how many e-mails you receive and send each day and what works best for you. We generally recommend that you process your e-mail two or three times a day.

| **Reflection Activity** | *When Are the Best Times for You to Process Your E-mail?* |

1. Do you process your e-mail in the early morning, mid-morning, lunch time, mid-afternoon, or late in the day?

2. Do you block out regular times?

3. When do others in your e-mmunity send their e-mails?

4. Are you timing your processing to catch large blocks of incoming messages?

5. If you share a computer with other people, how do you work out your schedule with theirs?

3. Decluttering

The third function in an e-mail management system is decluttering, which involves getting rid of e-mails from your mailbox, including in box, sent items, and deleted items. Decluttering also means not creating unnecessary, long, unclear, or misguided messages in the first place. Decluttering keeps your file storage space under control and ensures that all messages sent will further a purpose.

The purpose of decluttering is to clear the piles away so you and others can focus on getting things done. Decluttering practices will keep your own mailbox tidy and help keep your e-mmunities' messages less cluttered.

Decluttering is an ongoing function. To keep files decluttered, periodically purge obsolete files and archive inactive files.

THE FIRST FUNCTION OF AN E-MAIL SYSTEM IS *ORGANIZING*

Organizing e-mail involves creating categories for storing or filing then setting routines and making those routines into habits.

Most people who use computers at work already organize and keep information filed on their PCs and in their paper files. Some people also use shared files that are kept on the organization's computer network and paper file rooms.

Your "System" Files

When you get e-mail with information you need to keep, you must first decide which set of files to store the information in. Ask yourself:

- Should I print a copy to add to my paper files?

- Should I store the information in my own computer files?

- Should I print a copy to add to our shared paper files?

- Should I store the information on the network in a shared file for other people in the organization to access?

We will offer more on how to use your system files in the next section on *processing*, the second function of managing the barrage of e-mail.

For your filing system to work, you must make sure your electronic computer files align with or complement the files you have created in your paper files and your shared files. You may have to recategorize files in one or all of those places to get organized.

To organize your e-mail files, you must first create the file categories or folders for storing information that has been sent to you. Then you can organize your existing "in box" information and "sent messages" into your new folders. Some e-mail software will even allow you to use filters or rules automatically to sort your e-mail into folders.

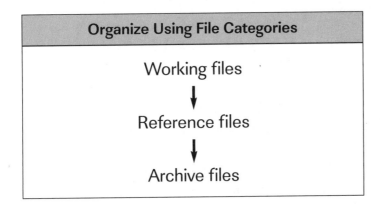

We suggest you organize your paper and electronic files by using the following categories:

☑ **Working Files**—paper and electronic files you use frequently to perform normal work functions. Create folders to hold your working files, which may include:

- Contact information for customers, vendors, employees
- Calendars or schedules, to do lists, project plans
- Routine files—trips, meetings, staff
- Current projects
- Tickler or hold file
- Alphabetized files
- Reading
- Action items
- "Hot" files—top priority or urgent projects, legally/financially sensitive information, VIP clients

☑ **Reference Files**—paper and electronic files you, use for special projects. Create folders to hold your reference files, which may include:

- Research information
- Past projects
- Resource information
- Personnel
- Administrative
- Budget
- Accounts
- Ideas
- Catalogs, reading
- Pending projects

☑ **Archive Files**—paper and electronic files you no longer use.

- Inactive files that have historical or legal significance
- Storage is based on document retention guidelines and policies

Application Activity	*Organizing Your E-mail Files*

Using the Tiptionary: Checklist for Organizing E-mail in the Tools & Tips section, take this time to organize your e-mail files into folders.

THE SECOND FUNCTION OF AN E-MAIL SYSTEM IS *PROCESSING*

Processing e-mail involves using the 4 R's (Read, Respond, Review, Revisit), the 4 S's (Scan, Skim, Study, Sort), the 5 D's (Delete, Delegate, Do now, Delay (do later), Dock (file)), and the 2 F's (Follow through and Follow up.)

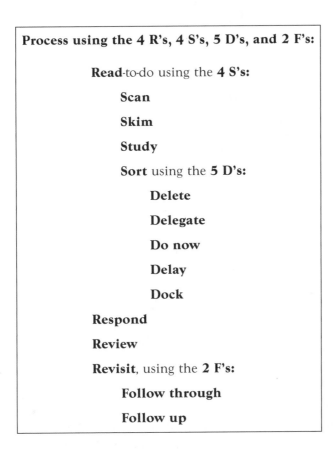

Process using the 4 R's, 4 S's, 5 D's, and 2 F's:

    Read-to-do using the **4 S's:**

        Scan

        Skim

        Study

        Sort using the **5 D's:**

            Delete

            Delegate

            Do now

            Delay

            Dock

    Respond

    Review

    Revisit, using the **2 F's:**

        Follow through

        Follow up

The 4 R's. The 4 R's are major steps in processing your e-mail:

1. **Read-to-do** using the 4 S's and the 5 D's. Processing your e-mail is unlike most of the **reading-to-learn** we were trained for in school. The purpose of this kind of reading is to remember information that we may retrieve at another time. In school, we were supposed to remember information to participate in class discussions, to pass tests, or to use sometime later in life.

Reading e-mail requires more of a **reading-to-do** focus—reading to determine the actions required to fulfill your goals or purpose. This kind of reading is supposed to help us complete tasks and then let go. We do not have to retain unnecessary information and clutter our brains. We do not have to read everything we receive, and we do not have to read everything contained in messages we do receive.

When we process e-mail, we do not have to remember all the information. Instead, the e-mail either prompts us to complete a task or archive information that we can find and act on later. We have categorized e-mail reading-to-do into the 4 S's found in a following section.

2. **Respond.** After reading all of your e-mails and deciding what to do, you move on to *respond*. Of course, you do not have to respond to every e-mail you receive. When you decide which e-mails require a response, you can draft your response by:

   - Greeting the sender
   - Identifying yourself
   - Answering any questions asked
   - Fulfilling any requests
   - Asking questions you have
   - Making requests you have, including purpose, expected results, responsibilities, specific tasks, and deadlines
   - Anticipating anything else the sender might need

   You may want to dedicate a block of time to respond to all correspondence at the same time. Look for a quiet time without interruptions so you can concentrate and give your responses the attention they deserve.

3. **Review.** After drafting your response, *review* your response by:

   - Proofreading your message
   - Asking a peer to edit your message
   - Predicting the outcome and making necessary adjustments to the message. Anticipate how the message will land with the customer and compose the message so it lands well

4. **Revisit.** After reviewing and sending your response, *revisit* by using the 2 F's in a following section.

The 4 S's. The 4 S's are four levels of reading. *Scanning* the header and *skimming* the body of the message allows you to preview to get an idea of the importance of each message without having to read everything at first. If the message merits additional attention, you move on to *study* content for appropriate actions and *sort* to handle paperwork, scheduling, and work assignments.

1. **Scan** the header and note:

   - *Whom* is the message from? Is the message from an individual or is it a newsletter or from a listserv?

- *What* is the subject of the message? Does this e-mail contain a new message or is this e-mail a response to a message I have already sent? Is this something that merits my time or should I delete the message?

- *When* was the message sent and when should I deal with it? Is it marked or does it seem to be high priority?

2. **Skim** the body of the message and decide:

   - *Why* was the message sent?

   - How important is this message? Should I delete it?

3. **Study** the message and decide:

   - *How* should I deal with the message?

   - What actions do I need to focus on? How do these actions serve the sender? How do they fit with our business goals and objectives? How do they contribute to the organization?

4. **Sort** the message using the **5 D's.**

The 5 D's. The 5 D's require being decisive and choosing one of the following to keep your e-mails flowing and generating appropriate actions. In the medical field, they call it "triage"—sorting and prioritizing to be sure the most important "cases" are handled first.

1. **Delete?** When *sorting*, your first decision is whether to *delete*. Remember: You do not have to read everything you receive, and you do not have to read everything contained in the messages you do read. To get rid of incoming messages that do not help you fulfill your purpose, functions, or tasks, ask yourself:

   > *"On forwarded e-mail: 'You say delightful, I say deleteful.'"*
   > –Fox, 1999

   - Do I need to keep it at all?

   - Learn to say "No!"

2. **Delegate?** If you do not delete the e-mail, your next decision is whether to delegate. You may delegate the entire task or sub-tasks, such as information gathering, research, problem solving, and decision making. Make sure you follow up to ensure follow through. Ask yourself:

   > *"Three quarters of all e-mail is of no practical use. Up to half of it is deleted without being read."*
   > –Fastrak, 1999

   - Can someone else do it?

   - If so, decide and communicate who, what, why, the intended result, details and information required, standards, and checkpoints before you delegate.

3. **Do Now?** If you did not delete or delegate the message, your next decision is whether you *do now*. Ask yourself:

   - If it would take *less than 2 minutes* to do, do it immediately.

   - If it would take *more than 2 minutes*, do it later today. Remember to add it to your "to do" or task list for the day. When you schedule tasks, remember to perform similar tasks together.

■ If it truly requires an *immediate response*, do it immediately. Reserve immediate responses for messages that are both urgent and important. Urgent messages require immediate attention. Important messages require action that contributes to the collective purpose and aligns with organizational mission, values, and goals.

4. **Delay?** If you are not going to *do now*, decide if you will *delay* it:

■ Do it later (after today)?

■ Schedule it. Commit to an action or set of actions in your calendar, project plan, contact manager, or tickler file.

5. **Dock?** If you are not doing to delete, delegate, do now, or delay the message, you may want to *dock* or file it. Ask yourself:

■ Do I need to keep this on file?

■ Where should I file it?

■ Remember to back up your files periodically.

> *"Imagine you're starting your day at your desk and you have 57 e-mails and it's only 8:45 a.m. Which ones do you open first? If you have no idea what they are about, you will probably save the 'No Subject' e-mails for last. We know we do."*
>
> –Chase and Trupp, 2000

The 2 F's—Follow through and Follow up. After you have written and sent your *response*:

1. **Follow through** by making sure you complete any promises you make.

2. **Follow up** on your own assignments and any that you delegated to others until you are sure the sender's needs have been met or exceeded.

Use your calendar, project plan, contact manager, or tickler file system to schedule your *follow-through* and *follow-up* actions.

As you follow through on your actions, remember to write e-mails and other communications that help your recipient focus on actions that fulfill your common purpose.

Reflection Activity   *Follow through and Follow up*

What have you done on e-mail today that requires follow through and follow up?

Application Activity	*Reading to Do Using the 4 S's and the 5 D's*

Using the Tiptionary: Checklist for Processing E-Mail, open your e-mail in box and read-to-do. If you have any responses to write, use the checklist to guide you.

When you get ready to draft a response, look through the chapter on writing e-mail to help you compose your message.

Before sending your e-mail, use the review section of the checklist.

Finally, don't forget to revisit to track or schedule follow-through and follow-up actions.

THE THIRD FUNCTION OF AN E-MAIL SYSTEM IS *DECLUTTERING*

The third function in an e-mail management system is decluttering, which involves getting rid of e-mails from your mailbox. Decluttering also means not creating unnecessary, long, unclear, or misguided messages in the first place. Decluttering keeps your file storage space under control and ensures that all messages sent will further a purpose. The purpose of decluttering is to clear the piles away so you and others can focus on getting things done.

Decluttering is an ongoing function. We recommend that you set up a time periodically to purge and archive your e-mails, again depending on how many you receive and send each day. How often you clear your mailbox may also depend on your organization's policy on e-mail: what must be kept, what must be legally documented, and how often your e-mails must or will be deleted. Of course, we recommend that you learn how to write e-mails effectively and responsibly so you will not create inefficient communications. We also recommend that you practice Netiquette and do not send unnecessary or inappropriate messages.

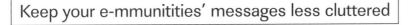

Declutter by Limiting the Flow
Keep your own mailbox tidy ↓ Keep your e-mmunitities' messages less cluttered

The following decluttering practices will **keep your own mailbox tidy.**

■ **Limit the inflow.** Ask: do I need this? You may want to request to be taken off some distribution lists, limit subscriptions to listservs and newsgroups, and use spam filters to cut back on unsolicited junk e-mail.

■ **Keep things moving.** Keep your in box clear or decide on a reasonable number of e-mails you keep as tickler items by processing your e-mails two to three times per day. Determine the proper routing, place, and schedule. You may want to create distribution lists but use them judiciously.

- **Limit the outflow.** Ask: do I really need to send this? Only send messages that further the recipient's purpose and actions. Limit forwarding messages.

- **Put things where they belong.** Keep your in box processed and clear. File what you need to keep in the appropriate "hard" or "soft" file. Save e-mail addresses for followup.

- **Consolidate.** If you have more than one mailbox or account, find out how you can use your e-mail software to collect mail in one place/location for processing.

- **Filter.** Know your e-mail software and how to use "filters" or "rules" to route messages to appropriate folders. You can filter incoming messages of known addresses or subjects to specific files for separate processing. You can use this function to send lower priority or junk messages to separate folders, which can be processed separately or deleted.

- **Purge.** Empty your recycle bin or deleted mail folder frequently—daily or weekly, depending on the number of e-mail messages you process. Clean out your hard and soft files one to four times a year, depending on how much information you process.

The following decluttering practices will keep your *e-mmunities' messages less cluttered.*

- Know your company's e-mail policy.

- Focus on purpose and actions. Limit each e-mail to one topic per message. Tell the recipient why he or she received the e-mail, what action you are requesting, and by when.

- Write clear, concise, and complete messages with descriptive, focused, subject lines. You may want to use standard formats generated by your organization or team.

- Limit your use of CC'ing and the "Reply to All" button.

- Limit attachments. Again, make sure they further the recipient's purpose and actions. Can the recipient handle the number of attachments? The file size? The type of file or software version?

- Stay within your disk size limits.

- Avoid spamming, jamming, and flaming. Do not spread hoaxes and forward other spam or jam. Use spam filters to cut down on unsolicited junk e-mail. Delete spam you do receive. Do not respond to spam. Responding only verifies that they have a valid address and encourages more spam. Learn to request nicely that others not send you jam (if you do not want to receive it). Do not post your e-mail address while on the Web.

- Use antivirus software to protect your system.

- Limit the size and frequency of messages.

■ Cut down on large distributions and forwarding by using public folders, groupware, project databases, public calendar/events, or a humor database as a central location for frequently accessed information.

■ Notify others when you are away. Post when you will return and whom to contact if they have an emergency.

Reflection Activity	*Keeping Your Mailbox and Your E-mmunities Mailboxes Tidy*

1. What decluttering activities do you already do?

2. What are some additional decluttering activities you can put into practice right away?

TOOLS & TIPS

Hot Tools & Tips!

The remaining pages in this chapter contain a quiz and job guides such as tips, checklists, and references.

✔	**QUICK CHECK***

1. To communicate effectively and responsibly, each communication must align with the organization's purpose, policy, and _____.

2. What are the three functions of an e-mail management system?

3. Name the 4 S's of processing.

4. Name the 5 D's of sorting.

5. The 2 F's of processing are follow through and follow up.   True or False?

6. What is the difference between scanning and skimming your e-mail?

7. What are three ways to keep your own e-mailbox decluttered?

8. A way to keep your e-mmunities' messages less cluttered is to avoid spamming, jamming, and flaming.   True or False?

9. A good e-mail practice is to notify others when you are away.   True or False?

10. Business communications do not need to further collective purpose and align with the mission and goals of a business.   True or False?

*Turn to page 155 for answers to the Quick Check.

WOW (Words of Wisdom)

Managing the Barrage of E-mail

1. Always use effective time and information management strategies to get a handle on communication overload.

2. To communicate effectively and responsibly at work, make sure each communication aligns with your organization's purpose, policy, and protocol.

3. To manage the barrage of e-mail use a three-part system:
   - organizing
   - processing
   - decluttering

4. Organize e-mail into working, reference, and archive files.

5. Process using the 4R's, 4S's, 5D's, and 2F's.

6. After you have determined the appropriate actions to take, be sure to follow through and follow up to fulfill your common purposes.

7. Follow decluttering practices to keep your mailboxes tidy and help keep your e-mmunities' mailboxes less cluttered as well.

Tiptionary	*Checklist for Organizing E-mail*

Organize your paper and electronic files by using the following categories:

- [ ] **Working Files**
    - [ ] Contact information for customers, vendors, employees
    - [ ] Calendars or schedules, to do lists, project plans
    - [ ] Routine files—trips, meetings, staff
    - [ ] Current projects
    - [ ] Tickler or hold file
    - [ ] Alphabetized files
    - [ ] Reading
    - [ ] Action Items
    - [ ] "Hot Files"
- [ ] **Reference Files**
    - [ ] Research information
    - [ ] Past projects
    - [ ] Resource information
    - [ ] Personnel
    - [ ] Administrative
    - [ ] Budget
    - [ ] Accounts
    - [ ] Ideas
    - [ ] Catalogs, reading
    - [ ] Pending projects
- [ ] **Archive Files**
    - [ ] Inactive files that have historical or legal significance
    - [ ] Storage is based on document retention guidelines and policies

☐ **Read**-to-do using the 4 S's and the 5 D's:

  ☐ **Scan** the header and note:

    ☐ *Who* is the message from?

    ☐ *What* is the subject of the message?

    ☐ *When* was the message sent and *when* should I handle it?

  ☐ **Skim** the body of the message and decide:

    ☐ *Why* was the message sent?

    ☐ Should I pay attention to this e-mail?

  ☐ **Study** the message and decide:

    ☐ *How* should I deal with the message?

    ☐ *What* actions do I need to focus on?

  ☐ **Sort** using the 5 D's

    ☐ Delete?

    ☐ Delegate?

    ☐ Do now?

    ☐ Delay?

    ☐ Dock?

☐ **Respond**

  ☐ Greet the sender.

  ☐ Identify yourself.

  ☐ Answer any questions asked.

  ☐ Fulfill any requests.

  ☐ Ask questions you have.

  ☐ Make requests you have, including purpose, expected results, responsibilities, specific tasks, and deadlines.

  ☐ Anticipate anything else the sender might need.

☐ **Review**

  ☐ Proofread using checklists.

  ☐ Peer edit.

  ☐ Predict the outcome and adjust the message.

☐ **Revisit** using the 2 F's:

  ☐ Follow through?

  ☐ Follow up?

Tiptionary	*Checklist for Decluttering E-mail*

Practices to keep your own mailbox tidy:

☐ Limit the inflow.

☐ Keep things moving.

☐ Limit the outflow.

☐ Put things where they belong.

☐ Consolidate.

☐ Filter.

☐ Purge.

Practices to keep your e-mmunities' messages less cluttered:

☐ Know company's e-mail policies.

☐ Focus on purpose and actions.

☐ Write clear, concise, and complete messages.

☐ Limit use of CC'ing and "Reply to All".

☐ Limit attachments.

☐ Stay within your disk size limits.

☐ Avoid spamming, jamming, and flaming.

☐ Use antivirus software to protect your system.

☐ Cut down on large distributions and forwarding.

☐ Notify others when you are away.

Key Terms

Reading-to-do
Reading-to-learn

References

Armour, S. (1999, March 2). E-mail 'helps' bog down workers. *USA Today*. Available: www.usatoday.com/life/cyber/tech/cte524.htm [1999, March 2].

Baker, L. and Douglass, M. (1993.) *Time mastery profile: How to manage your time more effectively*. Minneapolis: Carlson Learning Company.

Beardsley, D. (1998, April-May). Don't manage time, manage yourself. *Fast Company*, 64, 66.

Berst, J. (1999, September 7). Cut your e-mail in half. *ZDNet*. Available: www.zdnet.com/chkpt/adem2fpt/www.anchordesk.com/story/story_3817.html [1999, September 3].

Berst, J. (1999, September 19). The hidden spam problems (and how to stop it). *ZDNet*. www.zdnet.com/anchordesk/story/story_3489.html [1999, September 19].

Chase, M. and Trupp, S. (2000). *Office e-mails that really click*. Newport: Aegis Publishing Group, Ltd.

Covey, S. R. (1989). *The 7 habits of highly effective people*. New York: Fireside.

Crowley, A. (1999, July 5). Mail's got you. *PC Week*, 57–60.

Daily e-mail output to reach 35 billion. (2000, October 12). *Nua Internet Surveys*. Available: www.nua.ie/surveys [2001, June 6].

E-mail—boon or burden? (1999, October 15). *Fastrak Consulting*. Available: www.fastrak-consulting.co.uk/tactix/Features/e-mail/mail02.htm [1999, October 15].

E-mail boosts employee productivity. (2000, May 26). *Nua Internet Surveys*. Available: www.nua.ie/surveys [2001, June 6].

Fox, M. (1999, May 16). When e-mailers re-mail: The tedium is the message. *Seattle Times*. Available: www.seattletimes.com/news/lifestyles/htm198/fox_19990516.html [1999, May 19].

Gleeson, G. (1998). *The high-tech personal efficiency program*. New York: John Wiley & Sons.

Leonard, A. (1999, September 20). We've got mail—always. *Newsweek*, 58–61.

Lewis, J. (1999, April 11). Organize to avoid information overload. *National Seminars*. Available: www.natsem.com/9802.html [1999, April 11].

Mindell, P. (1993). *Power reading*. Upper Saddle River, NJ: Prentice Hall.

Newman, H. (1998, December 20). E-mail tricks: just filter it, then file it. *Detroit Free Press Online*. Available: www.freep.com/tech/pcathome/qnewmanzol.htm [1999, December 20].

Ogden, C. A. (1999, October 15). Internet tricks of effective e-mail users. *Deepwoods*. Available: www.deepwoods.com/Transform/pubs/E-mail/Tricks.htm [1999, October 15].

Soukhanov, A.H. (Ed.). (1992). *The American heritage dictionary of the English language* (3rd ed.). Boston: Houghton Mifflin Co.

Swamped workers switch to 'unlisted' e-mails. (1999, September 8). *USA Today*. Available: www.sjmercury.com/svtech/news/breaking/merc/docs/085259.htm [1999, September 6].

Take control of your e-mail system. (1999, March 9). *Ragan's Intranet Report.* Available: www.ragan.com/newsletter/Article_IR_2366.html [1999, March 9].

Whyte, D. (1994). *The heart aroused.* New York: Doubleday/Currency.

Whurman, R. S. (2001). *Information anxiety 2.* Indianapolis, IN: Que.

Winston, S. (1994). *The organized executive.* New York: Warner.

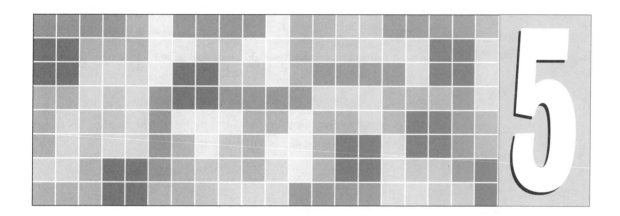

The Heart and Soul of E-Service: Using E-mail to Enhance Customer Service

"E-mail is one of the fastest ways to attract or lose customers because it delivers information fast to a single person or a mass of people."

—Chris McClean, 1999

WHAT YOU'LL LEARN IN THIS CHAPTER

Goal

- To present the Heart and Soul of E-Service Process for communicating with customers through e-mail

Objectives

As a result of this training, you should be able to:

- Apply Netiquette, e-mail writing, e-mail management, and customer service skills to provide excellent customer service through e-mail

- Put a person behind e-mails you send by adding heart and soul

- Handle difficult e-mails

- Compose e-mail messages that have the intended effect and affect when customers receive them

- Connect with your customers and build loyal partnerships

- Use e-mail communications as opportunities to support or help define your customer relationship management (CRM) strategies

---

ASSESS YOUR E-SERVICE E-MAIL QUOTIENT (EQ)

Check ☑ the following statements that describe how you use e-mail to provide customer service.

☐ 1. Have you ever responded to a customer's complaint without acknowledging their frustration or apologizing?

☐ 2. Do you ever send e-mails using templates, boilerplates, standard responses, or form letters without doing anything to personalize the message?

☐ 3. Have you ever sent confidential customer information through e-mail?

☐ 4. Have you ever sent an e-mail to a customer when you were angry or upset without worrying about the image you might be portraying?

☐ 5. Do you ever forget to follow up with a customer about their e-service?

☐ 6. Have you ever felt you could have handled e-mail to a difficult customer better?

☐ 7. Do you communicate with customers through e-mail without using a planned process?

☐ 8. Have you ever lost a customer due to a miscommunication through e-mail?

☐ 9. Do you send e-mail messages without your contact information, including a phone number?

☐ 10. Do you take longer than 24 hours to respond to your customers' e-mails?

If you placed a check next to three or more of these questions, you probably need some pointers on providing quality customer service through e-mail.

Here begins your adventure of using e-mail to build loyal customer partnerships.

E-MAIL IS A POWERFUL CUSTOMER SERVICE TOOL

Customer relationships are the lifeblood of successful businesses, and how we communicate with customers is key to the relationships we create.

E-mail has become a killer app for dealing with customer inquiries and complaints and for sharing information. But understanding how e-mail can enhance customer service will ensure that e-mail stays the killer app instead of the app that kills—a deal . . . a relationship . . . a customer!

As organizations have realized the value of customer relations, they have committed energy and resources to improving their customer service. Some organizations use simple **contact management** strategies, and some companies have implemented elaborate **customer relationship management (CRM)** strategies and tools to strengthen customer relationships.

But whether you use a business card file, an interoffice contact list, a **Rolodex**, an e-mail address file, a customer database, a contact management software, or a full-blown CRM system, e-mail can powerfully support or help define the way you nurture and develop customer relationships for your business.

Many click (e-based) and brick (land-based) businesses are employing CRM software that manages automated e-mail and **templated** (standard) responses to handle customer communications. But CRM software—an electronic connection—has its limits. It does not let us connect with our customers in personal ways. We need to connect more deeply. We need the human touch. As Rosabeth Moss Kanter stated in her book, *Evolve!: Succeeding in the digital culture of tomorrow* (2001), "The Web is a great facilitator, enhancer, and multiplier, but it is not a substitute for personal relationships."

Connecting, touching another human being, serving another in an e-world is a huge challenge. Keeping the human—the heart and soul—alive when we are no longer face-to-face or voice-to-voice requires a conscious process.

When we communicate through e-mail, we have already lost the body language and facial expressions of a face-to-face meeting. We have even lost the voice inflection of a phone conversation. If we use a standardized or automated message, we stand the chance of obliterating the personal touch entirely, and most recipients know when no person was behind the message.

We understand that when an organization chooses to use e-mail **auto-responses**, the idea is ultimately to save time and money. Developing templates takes a lot of resources. The upfront costs for setting up a CRM system can be huge. But unhappy customers, miscommunications, and damaged reputations can cost even more.

Nick Usborne describes wooden and flat customer service responses in "How to be Human 101:" " . . . dragging and dropping

> " . . . the value of a firm is ultimately equal to the sum of the values of its customer relationships, and this sum can grow only through the acquisition, development, and retention of profitable customer relationships."
>
> –Wayland and Cole, 1997

> CRM (customer relationship management) solutions use " sales and marketing automation tools" and " . . . promise to analyze what you know about your customers, including their buying habits and their complaints, and use that knowledge to advance your business."
>
> –Connolly, 2001

> "Contact management" is the process of managing, tracking, and organizing contacts with your customers and potential customers . . . to record every important detail of any communication with customers."
>
> –Timm, 2001

> "Your software doesn't create the relationships. . . . Your people still have to create the relationships."
>
> –Stephen R. Pratt, in Gaither, 2001

prewritten replies . . . [results in] a real, live person . . . trying hard to impersonate a computer."

Customers want to know that warm, caring humans, not cold, aloof strangers are communicating with them. They certainly do not want to think they are being handled by a computer. Your customers want you to understand they live in a chaotic world, and they want you to make their lives easier. They want you to take them seriously, and above all, they want you to listen and communicate that you care and are there to serve them. If we breathe life into our e-mail communications—providing the person, the voice that serves—we will create the customer relationships our business needs to survive and thrive.

Reflection Activity — Differences Between Face-to-Face, Voice-to-Voice, and Screen-to-Screen Communication

Which communication channel do you think you are most effective using:

- In person meetings?

- Phone conversations?

- E-mail?

Why?

WE ALL SERVE CUSTOMERS AT WORK

So, how do we begin to create these relationships with customers? First, we need to identify who our customers actually are.

A customer can be someone who *buys* your products or services. A customer can be someone in another department who *uses* the product of your work to fulfill on theirs.

Your manager is your customer. Your employees are your customers. Your team members can be your customers.

As Timm (2001) states in his book, *Customer Service: Career Success Through Customer Satisfaction*, a customer is "any person with whom we exchange value."

Obviously, if your job title is "customer service representative," you serve customers. However, everyone in your organization serves customers—either internal or external.

The key to business success is creating an organization that serves—where service is so much a part of the organization's identity that customers are served by employees who are served from within. Every business communication should help fulfill this purpose—to serve the needs of customers. Most likely, you are using e-mail more and more to provide service to your customers.

> "The truth of the matter is that in a world where user experience dictates brand, customer service is your brand."
>
> –Zemke and Connellan, 2000

Even though the rest of this chapter will focus on communicating with external customers, you can use the principles, tools, and tips to enhance your e-mail communications with internal customers as well.

Reflection Activity   *Who Are Your Customers?*

1. Who are your customers?

2. Are they internal to the organization or external?

3. What communication channels do you use to serve their needs?

EVERY COMMUNICATION SHOULD SERVE TO BUILD LOYAL PARTNERSHIPS

Loyal customer partnerships provide two basic business benefits:

- Avoiding the costs of lost customers
- Attracting additional business from existing customers and referred customers

The Costs of Lost Customers

Acquiring and retaining good customers is key to growing a business. Losing and replacing a customer is very costly. Disgruntled ex-customers often spread the word about negative experiences through e-mail, chat rooms, **bulletin boards**,

> *"Disgruntled consumers are a hot commodity on the Internet, where a dozen or more sites have been competing to become the virtual soapbox of choice for tens of thousands of angry customers."*
>
> —Appelman, 2001

and **complaint sites** on the Internet, influencing others to avoid or abandon your business. We all know how quickly the word spreads through the Internet.

Finding customers to fill the gap left by ex-customers and others they influenced is expensive. As Timm (2001) illustrates, attracting a new customer costs five to six times more than keeping an existing customer.

When most people think about losing customers, they think primarily about losing external customers. Losing an internal customer is also costly—to you and to the organization.

- A customer from another department might go to an outside source for the service you provide internally.

- Staff might leave because they can no longer deal with your e-mail tirades.

- Disgruntled internal customers might tell others within the organization about their displeasure and affect your ability to serve others.

- Stories could spread about your team or department and affect your ability to obtain the budget dollars you need.

- Team members could forward offensive internal e-mails to people outside the organization, leading to lost external customers, bad press, or a hit to your stock prices.

Mending severed internal relationships and replacing lost staff members costs much more than keeping internal customers happy.

So why expend the effort to build loyal customer partnerships rather than ignore the possibility we are not serving them? Because loyal customers:

- Continue to buy your products and services

- Provide recommendations and referrals that help build your customer base

- Continue to choose you over your competitors

- Provide excellent feedback for continuous improvement

Creating internal customer partnerships provides equivalent benefits to your team or department. It's like the old adage says, "The more you give, the more you get." When others within the organization appreciate what you give, you receive their acknowledgment, support, and advocacy in return.

YOU CAN BUILD LOYAL CUSTOMER PARTNERSHIPS BY PROVIDING VALUE

Serving customers means providing value. Darren Allen, in "Serving e-Customers: One at a Time," lists four value propositions:

■ Offering a unique product or service

■ Saving the customer time and effort

■ Saving the customer money (or delivering a fair price)

■ Offering a unique experience (e.g., via **personalization**)

Providing value goes beyond the inherent value of the product or service you offer. As Nick Usborne (2001) states in "Add More Value to That Automated E-mail," you must "make [customers] feel that they are valued."

How do you use e-mail to communicate in a way that *values others and their needs*? By:

> *"Building customer relationships tops the list of favoured competition strategies, cited by 58 percent of all firms polled. Providing high value for buyers was next, cited by 52 percent."*
> —NUA, 2001

■ Understanding the good, the bad, and the ugly of **e-service** communications

■ Practicing good Internet etiquette (Netiquette)

■ Writing effective and responsible e-mail

■ Managing your e-mail communications

THE GOOD, THE BAD, AND THE UGLY OF E-SERVICE

Chapter 1, "E-mail: The Good, the Bad, & the Ugly," presented the advantages and disadvantages of communicating through e-mail. In this section, we will look at how customer service delivered over e-mail can be good, bad, or downright ugly.

Reflection Activity   *The Good of E-Service*

1. As a customer, what e-mails have you received that offered something of value to you?

2. As a customer service representative or an internal service provider, what are some effective ways you have used e-mail in your organization?

Reflection Activity   *The Bad of E-Service*

1. As a customer, what e-mails have you received that offered nothing but problems?

2. As a customer service representative or an internal service provider, what problems were created or made worse through e-mail in your organization?

Reflection Activity   *The Ugly of E-Service*

1. What ugly e-service stories have you heard about or experienced?

2. As a customer, what e-mails have you received that converted you from a loyal to a lost customer?

3. As a customer service representative or an internal service provider, what e-mail communications created damaged customer relationships, caused you or your organization embarrassment, or created legal problems?

Today's savvy customers want to communicate in multiple ways, and e-mail is one of the most convenient. But convenient communications are more than fast and easy. They provide convenient *opportunities* to build loyal partnerships, to keep our customers informed, and to sell them something: ideas, services, and products. Every e-mail is an *opportunity*.

E-mail use and opportunities keep increasing. In response to the bio-terrorist scare of sending anthrax and other potentially lethal substances through the post office, people are turning to e-mail as the preferred method of communication. E-mail seems safer—it carries no bacteria. (But you still need to watch those viruses!) So now even more, people must learn to use e-mail effectively.

Jackie Gallogly and Lynne Rolls (2001) suggest how to use e-mail as a powerful one-to-one marketing and customer service tool:

- Send e-mail with a call to action; encourage recipients to respond by e-mail, phone, or fax.

- Send electronic invoices as a backup to mailed pieces. Ask customers if they want to **opt in** to e-mail billing only.

- If your mail delivery is slowing down and response time will be affected, use e-mail to effectively and rapidly communicate with customers. They may have sent you mail—or you may have sent them mail—but with slow delivery times and anxiety, who knows what was delivered or opened?

- Make e-mail an option for your customers. If you are a publisher, let people receive their subscriptions online. Give customers options; don't lose them while they are distracted.

- Send simple e-mail notifications and reminders to customers explaining ways they can communicate with you other than by postal service.

To shine and take advantage of the opportunity, knowing how to compose an effective e-mail is critical. Look at the following examples of good, bad, and ugly responses to this e-mail from a customer, Nancy D.

From the customer (Nancy D.) to Customer Service:

To:	Customer Service
Cc:	
Subject:	My order

I am still waiting to receive my CD, *Ava Rose Sings the Blues.* Is it out of stock?

Nancy D.

From Customer Service to the customer (Nancy D.)—ugly:

To:	Nancy D.
Cc:	
Subject:	My order

All out-of-stock orders are handled by customer service reps in our Chicago office.

Customer Service

From Customer Service to the customer (Nancy D.)—bad:

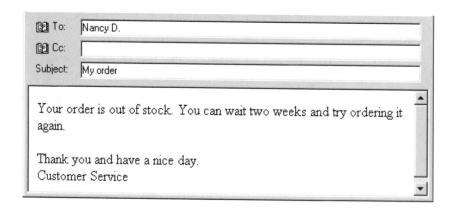

From Customer Service to the customer (Nancy D.)—good:

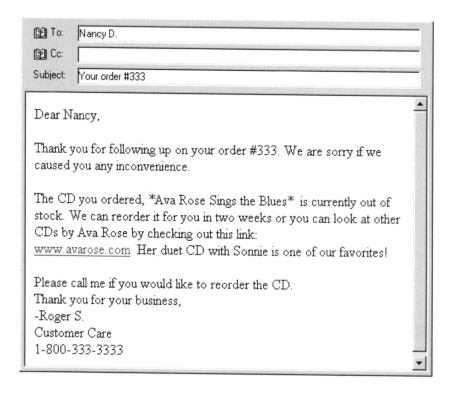

Application Activity

1. What makes the first customer service response ugly?

2. What makes the second response bad?

3. Why is the third response good?

WE SHOULD APPLY THE SIX NETIQUETTE GUIDELINES TO E-SERVICE

Chapter 2, "Business Netiquette: Being a Good E-mmunity Netizen at Work," presented six Netiquette guidelines to provide a map of how to be a good electronic community Internet citizen at work. This section links the Netiquette guidelines to quality customer service skills. Applying the six Netiquette guidelines to e-service will help you exceed customer expectations and build loyal customers.

1. Practice the "platinum rule for the new millennium."

Always treat others as they would have you treat them. With the "platinum rule," we flex to our customers' preferences, thus improving relationships and communications.

Excellent customer service communications reflect an attitude of service—providing an experience that builds customer satisfaction and loyalty. As with face-to-face and voice-to-voice customer service, electronic customer service must show:

- Respect
- Caring
- Compassion
- Generosity
- Empathy
- Reassurance

> "...the e-mail response is a transaction between customer and company that the customer can, and does, use to judge both the company concern for the customer's unique needs and problems and the company's responsiveness skills."
>
> –Zemke and Connellan, 2000

> "Communication experts have long recognized that (1) the more we know about our message receiver(s), and (2) the more we personalize a message to the receiver's wants and interests, the more effective we will be in communicating and building relationships."
>
> –Timm, 2001

Identifying and satisfying your customers' needs, including their need for a human touch, will earn your service a platinum award.

To practice the **platinum rule for the new millennium:**

- **Personalize your messages.**
    - **Put a person behind each message.** Be empathetic, caring, and *personable.*
    - **Use correct titles.** Some people become offended if you address them with the wrong title. Do your homework and make sure you get the most current information.
    - **Add a signature** or at the least sign your name and add your contact information to each e-mail you send. Make it easy for your customers to relate to you.

> *". . . e-mail allows marketers to craft a personalized message for each prospect. Instead of mass mailing identical messages, an e-mail can be tailored to a specific interest."*
>
> –Johnson, 2001

    - **Customize templated responses as often as you can.** Even if you use a templated response, make sure you personalize it. Embellish the template enough to have the customer think you wrote the message just for them. Customers recognize an autoresponse and often react poorly when they receive one. You may be able to handle some situations with an autoresponse or a template, but templates are not very often adequate responses. Remember, they serve as a starting point—to set standards and spark some ideas. If you have a good customer service attitude, if you add some heart and soul, you will figure out how to begin with that template and tailor it to fit the service you are fulfilling for your customer.

- **Know your customers' response time expectations and exceed them.** Because e-mail communication is so quick and easy to send, people expect a quick response. Optimal response time can vary depending on your type of business and your customers' needs. In an e-commerce business, customers may want a response time of one hour or less, but often respect a response of less than six hours. Jupiter Media Matrix reported (January 3, 2002) that "retailers struggled to respond to customers' requests online this [Christmas 2001] season." While customers expected a response within six hours, only 30 percent of retailers met their expectation. Other internal and external customers may expect a response within 24 hours.

    If your company has a response time policy, check to see what it is. Otherwise, learn your customers' response time expectations and work to exceed them.

- **Always acknowledge the customers' message.** A good rule of thumb for excellent customer service is *to be the person to finish the correspondence.* You should:

    - Confirm receipt of their messages if you need time to fix problems. Let the customers know you are owning the problems and what to expect in terms of time to solution.

☐ Assure them that you care and will champion their cause.

☐ Ask them if they need anything else from you.

☐ Provide them with any follow-up you promised.

☐ Be the last one to continue contact unless they tell you not to continue contact, be the last one to correspond. You are acknowledging their importance to you.

■ **Understand their need and exceed it.** "Listen" carefully as you read to identify your customers' needs and make sure you meet or exceed their expectations.

☐ Pay attention to address each concern they have.

☐ Answer every question they ask.

> "A recent study found that most consumers expect to get a response to their e-mail inquiry within six hours. Unfortunately, only 38% of companies are providing that kind of speedy service and 33% are taking three days or longer to respond. Even worse, 24% of companies do not respond to e-mail inquiries at all."
>
> –Tedeschi, 2001

Reflection Activity   *Practicing the Platinum Rule*

1. How can you "listen" for what your customers need—in terms of product, service, and heart-based treatment?

2. How can you monitor your own psychological reactions to your customers' e-mail? How can you be sure to avoid letting your psychological/emotional reactions adversely affect your writing tone?

3. How can you demonstrate the heart and soul of the organization by putting a person supported by a caring organization behind the message?

4. How can you avoid writing an e-mail that feels like a cold, automated response? How can you personalize your e-mail by adding a "voice" to standard responses (templates)?

Application Activity

Look at the last five e-mails you composed at work. What have you done well to practice the platinum rule? What more can you do?

2. Put "your best foot forward."

Customer service e-mail messages reflect on the writer and on the organization they represent. When you compose your message, be certain to project the appropriate image. You must write well and in a way that communicates what you and your organization stand for.

Your organization's brand is its mark of distinction in the marketplace. All communications, including customer service e-mails, must reflect your organization's brand image.

> "Branding is the total customer experience encompassing every step, from discovery to purchase to fulfillment to postpurchase service."
>
> –Zemke and Connellan, 2000

To practice **putting your best foot forward:**

■ **Write your response in a way that connects with the customer and projects the appropriate image of your organization.**

  ☐ Display your brand logo in your e-mails as you would use a letterhead in a business letter if you can.

  ☐ Include wording that conveys your brand. Create a pool of words and phrases that exemplifies the most important qualities your organization wants associated with its name. Use these words as often as you can in your e-mail messages.

  ☐ Consider using a standard closing or saying that the customer will learn to recognize as yours, even if your e-mails are just plain text (see the following). Southwest Airlines signs their e-mails "Luv." Their e-mails and the "Luv" signature support their commitment to be the "Luv Airline."

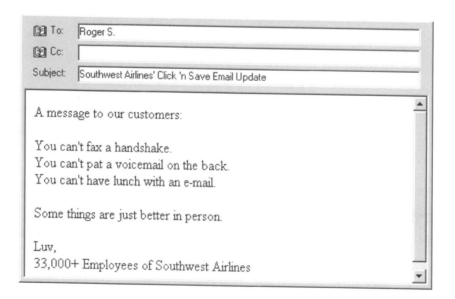

■ **Follow your organization's customer service and e-mail standards.**

  ☐ Learn the policies and procedures already in place for dealing with customer communications.

☐ Work continuously to improve e-mail response time and contact management systems.

■ **Check grammar, spelling, punctuation, and tone of your message.** Although being correct does not necessarily establish credibility, having errors in your e-mail will probably destroy your credibility.

■ **Write a clear, concise, and complete message.** If you take the time to be clear and complete, you can avoid having to write additional e-mails to straighten things out. Try to anticipate questions the reader may have and deal with those issues in your message up front.

■ **Add goodwill to each message.**

☐ Tell customers you value them.

☐ End all your messages on a positive note.

Reflection Activity   *Putting Your Best Foot Forward*

1. What image do you and your organization want to project? How can you improve your messages to reflect the desired image?

2. Think for a moment of some words and phrases you use or could use to describe your brand. Work with others within your organization to brainstorm a list. Keep this list handy to refer to when writing to customers about your brand.

Application Activity

Look at the last five e-mails you composed at work. What have you done well to put your best foot forward? What more can you do?

3. Nurture "harmonious connections."

Today's consumers are savvy. They have high expectations and are wary of being scammed, particularly in the e-world. Building and maintaining trust is critical to harmonious connections.

To practice **nurturing harmonious connections:**

- **Approach your customer with positive expectations and enthusiasm.** Be reliable, consistent, thorough, and trustworthy.

- **Use *you-attitude* and *can-do* language.** Tell customers what they can do rather than what they cannot do. Be responsive to their psychological and product/service needs.

  Remember, every communication is an opportunity to stay connected to your customer by providing value. Customer service communications that you can send to "connect" electronically include:

  - Alerts
  - Bill status
  - Current balances
  - Discounts or special offers
  - Expiration notices
  - Investor relations
  - New product availability
  - New product or service announcements
  - News flashes
  - Newsletters
  - Order confirmations
  - Promotions
  - Reports or white papers
  - Research
  - Reminders
  - Replenishment reminders
  - Requests for referrals
  - Shipping status
  - Surveys
  - Technical support
  - Thank you's
  - Traditional direct marketing campaigns
  - Transactions
  - Updates or changes
  - Web site links

> *You-attitude is a style of writing that looks at things from the reader's point of view, emphasizing what the reader wants to know, respecting the reader's intelligence, and protecting the reader's ego.*
>
> —Locker, 2000

> "*You need to 'wow' [customers] with your superior standards for quality and service. You must promote a feeling of partnership through honest sharing of information and respect for their needs and always build on a foundation of a trusting relationship. If you do these things, then you will build a loyal and profitable following online.*"
>
> —Zemke and Connellan, 2000

- **Make sure you fulfill on any actions you promise.** Remember, the good news and the bad news are that e-mail is such an easy way to communicate. When we rush to send an e-mail, we might make empty promises. But e-mail is a great way to do consistent follow through and follow up, which is key to good customer service. Always confirm if your customers received your messages and the messages met their needs.

- **Calm upset customers.** Serving an upset customer is an opportunity to build loyalty. Become an advocate for the customer and
  - ☐ Authentically express compassion for their frustration.
  - ☐ Apologize for the trouble.
  - ☐ Reassure them that you will help.
  - ☐ Help solve their problems.
  - ☐ Offer alternative solutions.
  - ☐ Offer something extra to compensate for their trouble.
  - ☐ Show that they are valued customers.

The following e-mail example illustrates calming an upset customer with can-do language and you-attitude:

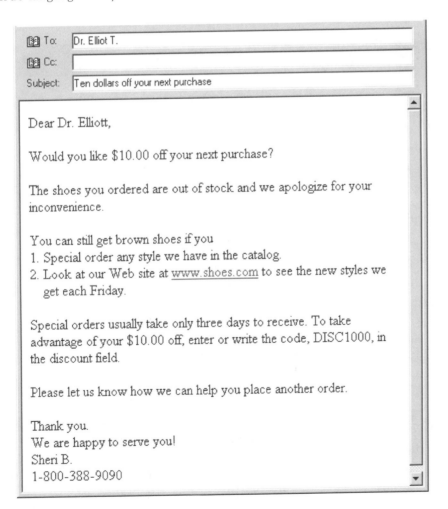

Reflection Activity   *Nurturing Harmonious Connections*

1. Think of a time when you or someone you know "connected" in an e-mail with another while helping meet their need. What did they do to create the connection?

2. When customers are upset, what can you do to compensate for their frustration and extra effort? What are your organization's guidelines on offering alternatives or something extra to a customer?

3. How can you use e-mail to serve your customers?

Application Activity

Look at the last five e-mails you composed at work. What have you done well to nurture harmonious connections? What more can you do?

---

4. Further "e-mmunity action."

"So shall my word be that goes out from my mouth; it shall not return to me empty, but it shall accomplish that which I purpose, and succeed in the thing for which I sent it."

—Isaiah 55:11

E-mail is an effective tool for communicating to make a difference for the customer, for the organization, and for the entire e-mmunity. All actions must further a purpose continuously to provide excellent customer service. Each customer communication has the potential to provide feedback for continuous improvement. Often, problems customers encounter are caused by system and technical issues. Customer service reps need latitude to fix problems and provide input into systems improvements.

To practice **furthering e-mmunity action:**

■ **Send focused messages that add value**. Do not forward jam and spam just because you can. Find out if customers want to hear from you and how often if you are sending e-mails that are not about their particular issue or order. Especially if you do not have a formal opt-in process, get permission or judge by their response whether or not to send them e-mail.

- **Own your customers' needs and problems.** Do what it takes to provide solutions and make sure to let them know how you are helping them.

- **Help customers take actions that make their lives easier.** Let them know what alternatives are available or what they can do to get what they need.

- **Provide contact information to help them communicate in their preferred way.** Do not make them work hard to figure out how best to reach you.

Reflection Activity   *Furthering E-mmunity Action*

1. Do you know what you can and cannot do for customers?

2. Do you have the product, service, and systems knowledge and skills to provide what your customers need?

3. Do you have permission to fix product, service, and systems problems? Do you have permission to compensate customers for the added costs of frustration and problem solving?

Application Activity

Look at the last five e-mails you composed at work. What have you done well to further e-mmunity action? What more can you do?

---

5. Travel "the straight and narrow."

Customer service communications must reflect your corporation's standards for communicating confidential and sensitive content in a legal and ethical manner. Compose your e-service communications to avoid spamming, flaming, jamming, violating copyright laws, ignoring security issues, and handling confidential or sensitive issues over e-mail.

To practice **traveling the straight and narrow:**

- **Follow your organization's e-mail policies and guidelines.** Find out what those policies and guidelines are and how they relate to customer service. If your organization does not have e-mail policies and guidelines, help your managers develop them.

- **Do not send sales solicitations without permission.** Get permission to send customers information about your products and services. Some customers appreciate e-mails that add value but get their permission to make sure. If you solicit them without their permission, you risk losing your credibility.

- **Avoid offensive language and jokes.** You are communicating to serve customers, not to amuse or offend them.

- **Cite copyrighted content.** If you copy any information, even information you found on the Internet, you must cite it properly.

- **Be careful not to send confidential information though e-mail.** Special pricing, credit card numbers, performance information, and other information that can be used in inappropriate ways have no place in e-mail. Handle confidential or sensitive information in person, on the phone, or over secured lines.

Reflection Activity   *Traveling the Straight and Narrow*

1. Do you know your organization's e-mail policies and guidelines? Do you know what customer information can be communicated electronically without violating confidentiality?

2. Do you include a way for customers to opt out of e-mail communications?

Application Activity

Look at the last five e-mails you composed at work. What have you done well to travel the straight and narrow? What more can you do?

6. Clean up the "neighborhood."

Responsible e-service Netizens keep the organization's and the customer's "neighborhood" clean by managing the barrage of e-mail. They "stay on purpose" by sending only e-mails that add value. They "keep the order" by systematizing, organizing, and decluttering their electronic communications.

To practice **cleaning up the neighborhood:**

- **Use a system to organize all customer contacts.** Use a paper-based or software-based system to keep track of interactions with your customers. Refer to your customer files to get a complete picture of how you can make their lives easier.

- **Keep your mailboxes, files, and databases tidy.** Process e-mails regularly. File e-mail and customer-related information where it belongs. Save e-mail addresses for follow-up. Archive or purge old or obsolete files.

- **Send only messages that add value and make the customer's life easier.** Always get permission and send files in formats your customers can read. Never send spam or jam. Limit the size and frequency of messages.

- **Do not send large attachments unless your customer's system can handle them.** Send only one attachment at a time unless you know you can send more. Many Internet service providers will not accept e-mail with more than one attachment or attachments that exceed a certain size.

    Cut back on providing information using attachments by providing the information on your Web site and including a clickable link to the information in your e-mail message.

Reflection Activity   *Cleaning Up the Neighborhood*

1. Do you have an organized way of tracking and managing customer contacts? Do you refer to customer files to understand fully their needs?

2. How frequently and consistently do you process customer e-mails? Do you follow up and follow through on promises?

Application Activity

Look at the last five e-mails you composed at work. What have you done well to clean up the neighborhood? What more can you do?

COMPOSING EFFECTIVE E-SERVICE MESSAGES REQUIRES A PROCESS

Chapter 3, "E-mail IS Business Writing: Composing Letters, Memos, and Notes at Work," presents some simple strategies for writing effective and responsible e-mail. This section shows you how to apply these strategies to compose e-mails that serve.

Effective customer service reps never underestimate the power of words to make or break a relationship. They use a process to compose their e-mail messages to get the result they intend. *Before writing,* they plan their message. *During writing,* they draft their message. *After writing,* they proofread and edit their message.

> *"E-mail littered with indecipherable sentences and grammatical errors or responses perceived by customers as abrupt, interpersonal, or condescending—a real danger with this mode of communication, because there's no body language or voice inflection to help interpret meaning—can do unseen harm to customer loyalty."*
>
> –Zemke and Connellan, 2000

Before Writing

- Identify the product or service needs of the customer
- Identify the psychological needs of the customer
- Identify and manage your own reactions to problems
- Check customer records for pertinent and accurate:
  - □ order information, including dates, order numbers, amounts, and descriptions
  - □ customer contact information
  - □ previous customer problems and communications
  - □ related issues with products and services
- Find appropriate solutions, actions, and information

Reflection Activity	*Before Writing*

1. What are some key words you can look for to identify your customer's product or service needs?

2. How can you interpret the tone of your customer's message to identify your customer's psychological needs?

3. After you have checked your own reactions to your customer's messages, how can you manage your own emotions and actions?

4. What customer records and internal staff do you have access to when researching your customer's needs and solutions?

During Writing

- Put a person behind each message.
- Greet the customer.
- Use correct titles.
- Capture the essence of your message in the subject line.
- Customize a proven templated response.
- Assure the customer that you care and will assist.
- Apologize, if appropriate.
- Use words that represent your brand image and value.
- Use *you-attitude* and *can-do* language.
- Answer all questions and address all concerns. Solve their problem or offer alternative solutions.
- Offer something extra to compensate for trouble, if appropriate.
- Confirm that the customer's needs have been met or exceeded.

- Invite an action to
  - ☐ place the order.
  - ☐ preserve the relationship.
- Recommend additional services and products that add value.
- Format your message for easy reading.
- Select a personal, thoughtful signoff.
- Add your signature with contact information so customers can communicate with you in their preferred way.
- Add attachments or links to valuable information, if appropriate.

Reflection Activity   *During Writing*

1. What are some ways you might greet your customer?

2. How might you identify yourself?

3. How can you show willingness to assist?

4. How can you show brand value to the customer?

5. How can you confirm that the customer's needs have been met?

After Writing

- Check spelling, punctuation, and grammar.
- Use the Tiptionaries in this book.
- Use the E-mail Style Guide in the Appendix.

- Verify the accuracy of all details.

- Predict the outcome and make necessary adjustments to the message.

- Be sure the message is organized and formatted to show you have handled all requests and concerns.

- Have an e-mail buddy or a peer edit for tone, readability, and completeness.

Reflection Activity	*After Writing*

1. What Tiptionary in Chapter 3, "E-mail IS Business Writing," can you use to *proofread* your message?

2. Who can you invite to be your e-mail buddy or peer editor?

3. Why is *predicting the outcome* of the e-mail so important?

PROVIDE E-SERVICE BY MANAGING YOUR E-MAIL COMMUNICATIONS

Chapter 4, "Managing the Barrage of E-mail," provided a system for organizing, processing, and decluttering your e-mail communications. This section shows you how to apply these strategies using our Heart and Soul of E-service Process.

Organizing

To provide excellent customer service, you must have a system for organizing customer-related transactions, including e-mail communications. Whether you use paper-based files, spreadsheets, databases, contact management software, or CRM systems, you need accurate, complete, and up-to-date records of your organization's interactions with your customers. Having organized records helps you answer customers' questions, solve their problems, and suggest value-added products and services by giving you access to information about your customers' order history, preference, and experiences with your organization.

Reflection Activity	*Organizing Customer Communications*

How do you track customer-related interactions? Is the information accurate? Complete? Up-to-date? Easy to access? Secure?

Processing

Using e-mail to meet needs and provide value requires a process that includes:

- **Reading-to-Do**—read to identify the needs of your customers—psychological and product/service.

- **Responding**—compose an e-mail that offers value and exceeds expectations.

- **Reviewing**—quality check your e-mail.

- **Revisiting**—follow through and follow up on promises and improvements.

Use the Tiptionaries at the end of this chapter to follow a proven method for processing your customer service e-mails. The Heart and Soul of E-Service Process Tiptionary pulls together Netiquette, writing, and e-mail management practices that result in excellent customer service communications. The Composing Effective E-Service Messages Tiptionary provides tips you can use before and during writing to respond to customer messages, as well as after writing tips you can use to review your e-mail messages.

Decluttering

Excellent customer service reps keep things in order by keeping their own and their customers' mailboxes tidy. They keep *their own mailboxes* tidy by processing, filing, and deleting. They want to make their customers' lives easier, so they help keep *their customers mailboxes* tidy by sending only messages that provide value. They never violate their customers' trust by barraging them with spam, jam, or sloppy messages.

CONTINUOUSLY IMPROVE YOUR E-SERVICE

To differentiate ourselves from our competitors, we must center our brand around extraordinary service.

Going beyond ordinary service to extraordinary service requires that we continuously improve our customer service. Because we are using e-mail more and more to connect with customers, improving our e-mail communications is key to improving our overall customer service.

E-mail gives us the opportunity to connect with customers for many reasons. We must always remember that each opportunity to connect is also an opportunity to disconnect.

This book has provided you with many tools and tips to improve your e-mail communications—to make sure you are communicating effectively and responsibly. We hope you will apply what you have learned to make sure each e-mail you send works.

> *"Clients view clear, precise communication skills as a sign of the company being confident, knowledgeable, and caring. A company that takes the time to present well-written material to a customer or client is showing responsibility."*
>
> –Locker, 2000

Application Activity

Add heart and soul to these autoresponses:

Dear Customer,

Thank you for your inquiry. While we attempt to answer as many e-mails as we can, we cannot answer every one. Please visit our Web site for more information.

Dear Customer,

I received your inquiry regarding the problems you're having with our product. Instead of my listing out a long series of instructions, I recommend that you visit our Web site to find a list of the common issues customers face along with places where you can find step-by-step instructions to fix them.

Application Activity   *Personal Commitment to Action*

Each of us must accept responsibility for improving customer service. As part of that responsibility, we need to be willing to take the actions necessary to enhance customer service using e-mail. Fill in this plan with the first three actions you will take to improve your e-service.

I will begin using what I have learned about The Heart and Soul of E-service Process by:

Action Item	Completion Date	Resources

Enjoy connecting with your customers!

Marcia Reed and Verna Terminello

TOOLS & TIPS

Hot Tools & Tips!

The remaining pages in this chapter contain a quiz and job guides such as tips, checklists, and references. You may want to cut these pages out and keep them at your desk for quick reference.

✔   **QUICK CHECK***

1. You should always identify yourself in an e-mail to a customer.   True or False?

2. You do not have to worry about personalizing your e-mails because customers assume you use templates.   True or False?

3. To bring your e-mail alive, you must add _____.

4. How do you practice peer editing of your e-mails?

5. Why should you supply your contact information?

6. Why should you provide your customer service phone number?

7. Why must you exceed customer expectations?

8. Why should you offer something extra when a customer reports a problem?

9. Why should you try to predict the outcome of your e-mail communication with a customer?

10. Why is it important to communicate in a way that is consistent with your brand?

*Turn to page 155 for answers to the Quick Check.

WOW (Words of Wisdom)

The Heart and Soul of E-service

1. Always remember to use the Heart and Soul of E-service Process when using e-mail for customer service.

2. Remember to add a voice to your e-mails so your customers know a person is behind each message you send.

3. Remember customers are interested in the "what's in it for me," so use you-attitude and can-do language in your messages to them.

4. Carefully choose the words, images, and feelings you want associated with the brand you represent.

5. Every e-mail correspondence with a customer is an opportunity and should work to build and maintain the relationship.

6. Know thy customers and be sincere and respectful with them. Don't forget—the competition is only a click away!

7. Although customers may not analyze your writing line by line, they will get a sense of a communication that is hurried, unclear, or sterile if you do not compose your messages mindfully.

8. Your e-mail becomes the salesperson, and you risk your credibility with each message you send.

9. Work with your e-mail buddy to help each other write effective and responsible e-mails.

10. Strive to make your company the Nordstrom of Cyberspace.

| **Tiptionary** | *The Heart and Soul of E-service Process* |

☐ **Read**—Determine your customers' needs and the actions required by using the 4 S's.

    ☐ **Scan**—The header for who (internal or external customer), what (subject or need), and when (date and time sent, urgency indicators).

    ☐ **Skim**—The body and decide why (psychological and product/service needs) and priority.

    ☐ **Study**—The message and decide how (actions required). Refer to customer records to fill in the gaps. Understand your policies, guidelines, standards, systems, processes, and procedures.

    ☐ **Sort**—The message by choosing how to handle the message using the 5 D's:

        ☐ **Delete**—If the message does not contain a need, you may choose to delete the message. Not every message requires a response. Some customer relationship management systems do not permit deleting messages, so you may file the message with a notation of no action required.

        ☐ **Delegate**—Ideally, you are empowered to do what it takes to serve the customer. When someone else is better equipped to make a difference, use their services to get results.

        ☐ **Do now**—Handle urgent issues immediately. If your system allows, perform similar tasks together.

        ☐ **Delay**—Confirm receipt of customers' messages quickly if you need time to fix problems. Respond with answers or solutions to customers' e-mail within 24 hours. Schedule actions to be handled later.

        ☐ **Dock**—Update customer files. Back up files periodically.

☐ **Respond**—Plan and draft your message.

    ☐ Use the before and during writing sections of the Composing Effective E-Service Messages Tiptionary.

☐ **Review**—Edit your message.

    ☐ Use the after writing section of the Composing Effective E-Service Messages Tiptionary.

☐ **Revisit**—Fulfill on promises and continuously improve processes.

    ☐ **Follow through**—Fulfill on promises by completing your own and others' scheduled actions. Confirm that the customers' needs have been met and you have exceeded their expectations.

    ☐ **Follow up**—Where appropriate, recommend additional services and products that add value. Update customer files. Use customer interactions to identify and implement improvements to your processes.

Tiptionary — *Composing Effective E-service Messages*

Before Writing—Plan your message.

- ☐ Identify product or service needs of customer.
- ☐ Identify psychological needs of customer.
- ☐ Identify and manage your own reactions to the problem.
- ☐ Check customer records for pertinent and accurate:
  - ☐ Order information, including dates, order numbers, amounts, and descriptions.
  - ☐ Customer contact information.
  - ☐ Previous customer problems and communications.
  - ☐ Related issues with products and services.
- ☐ Find appropriate solutions, actions, and information.

During Writing—Draft your message.

- ☐ Put a person behind each message.
- ☐ Greet the customer.
- ☐ Use correct titles.
- ☐ Capture the essence of your message in the subject line.
- ☐ Customize a proven templated response.
- ☐ Assure the customer that you care and will assist.
- ☐ Apologize, if appropriate.
- ☐ Use words that represent your brand image and value.
- ☐ Use *you-attitude* and *can-do* language.
- ☐ Answer all questions and address all concerns. Solve their problem or offer alternative solutions.
- ☐ Offer something extra to compensate for trouble, if appropriate.
- ☐ Confirm that the customer's needs have been met or exceeded.
- ☐ Invite an action to:
  - ☐ place the order.
  - ☐ preserve the relationship.
- ☐ Recommend additional services and products that add value.
- ☐ Format your message for easy reading.

☐ Select a personal, thoughtful signoff.

☐ Add your signature with contact information so customers can communicate with you in their preferred way.

☐ Add attachments or links to valuable information, if appropriate.

After Writing—Proofread and edit your message.

☐ Check spelling, punctuation, and grammar.

☐ Use the Tiptionaries in this book.

☐ Use the E-mail Style Guide in the Appendix.

☐ Verify the accuracy of all details.

☐ Predict the outcome and make necessary adjustments to the message.

☐ Be sure the message is organized and formatted to show you have handled all requests and concerns.

☐ Have an e-mail buddy or peer edit for tone, readability, and completeness.

Tiptionary	*Ways to Provide Value-Added Communications Through E-mail*

☐ Alerts

☐ Bill status

☐ Current balances

☐ Discounts or special offers

☐ Expiration notices

☐ Investor relations

☐ New product availability

☐ New product or service announcements

☐ News flashes

☐ Newsletters

☐ Order confirmations

☐ Promotions

☐ Reports or white papers

☐ Research

☐ Reminders

☐ Replenishment reminders

☐ Requests for referrals

☐ Shipping status

☐ Surveys

☐ Technical support

☐ Thank you's

☐ Traditional direct marketing campaigns

☐ Transactions

☐ Updates or changes

☐ Web site links

Key Terms

Acknowledgment

Attachments

Autoresponse

Bulletin board

Complaint site

Contact management

Customer relationship management
(CRM)

E-service

Opt in

Personalization

Rolodex

Template

References

ActivMedia. (2001, May 29). CRM key to profitability for online firms. *NUA*. www.nua.ie/surveys/index.cgi?f= VS&art_id = 905356812&rel= true [2001, June 6].

Allen, D. (2001, June 6). The expensive online customer. *eMarketer*. www.emarketer. com/analysis/ecommerce_b2c/20010606_b2c.html? ref=dn [2001, June 6].

Allen, D. (2001, June 13). Serving e-customers: One at a time. *eMarketer*. www. emarketer.com/analysis/ecommerce_b2c/20010613_b2c.html? ref=dn [2001, June 13].

Appleman, H. (2001, March 4). I scream, you scream: Consumers vent over the Net. *New York Times*. www.nytimes.com/2001/03/0-4/technology/04COMP.html [2001, March 4].

Blankenhorn, D. (2000, March 28). E-mail is never free. *ClickZ Network*. www.clickz. com/cgi-bin/gt/cz/cz.html? article=1502 [2000, March 28].

Blankenhorn, D. (2000, April 28). Customer service pays for itself. *Clickz Network*. www. clickz.com/cgi-bin/gt/cz/ebrl/ebr.html? article=1650 [2000, April 28].

Bolman, L. G. and Deal, T. E. (2001). *Leading with soul: An uncommon journey of spirit.* San Francisco, CA: Jossey-Bass.

Brooks, K. (2001, December 11). Lessons in customer service from the Web. *ClickZ Network*. www.clickz.com/cgi-bin/gt/cz/article.html? article=2993 [2001, December 11].

Burke, K. (1999, April 7). Top 10 tips on writing e-mail that sells. *ClickZ Network*. www.clickz.com/cgi-bin/gt/cz/cz.html? article=213 [1999, April 7].

Butler, S. (2001, February 2). The road ahead for B2B eCommerce. *eMarketer*. www.emarketer.com/analysis/ecommerce_b2b/20010202_top-ten_b2b.html? ref=dn [2001, February 4].

Carton, S. (2000, May 3). The secret to e-business success. *ClickZ Network*. www.clickz. com/cgi-bin/gt/cz/cz.html? article=1666 [1999, May 3].

Connolly, P. J. (2001, April 9). Can CRM win and retain loyal, repeat customers? www. findarticles.com/cf_o/moIFW/16-23/73281313/p1/article.jhtm? term=CRM [2002 January 7].

Cooper, C. (1999, December 8). Where is the Nordstrom of cyberspace. *ZDNet*. www.zdnet.com/zdnn [1999, December 8].

DeBellis, M. A. (1999, November 23). Customer disservice on the rise. *Red Herring.* www.herring.com/inside/1999/1123/vc-survey.html [1999, November 23].

Gaither, C. (2001, October 1). Software to track customers' needs helped firms react. *New York Times.* www.nytimes.com/2001/10/01/technology/ebusiness/01CRM.html [2001, October 1].

Gallogly, J. and Rolls, L. (2001, October 30). E-mail's opportunity to shine. *ClickZ Network.* www.clickz.com/em_mkt/em_mkt/print.php/911971 [2001, October 30].

Jaffe, J. (2001, September 18). Connecting with the reader. *ClickZ Network.* www.clickz.com/crm/connect/article.php/885891 [2001, September 18].

Johnson, J. (2001, February 5). Getting personal. *eMarketer.* www.emarketer.com/analysis/e-mail_marketing/20010205_e-mail.html? ref=dn [2001, February 5].

Johnson, J. (2001, April 30). The enemy within. *eMarketer.* www.emarketer.com/analysis/e-mail_marketing/20010430_e-mail.html? ref=dn [2001, May 22].

Jupiter Media Matrix. (2002 January 3). Retailers struggled to respond to customers' requests online this holiday season. Jupiter Media Matrix. www.jmm.xp/jmm/press/2002/pr_010302.xml [2002, January 4].

Kane, M. (2000, May 2). E-tailers: Make your customers happy. *ZDNet.* www.zdnet.com/zdnn/stones/news/0,4586,2560159,00.html? chkpt=zdhpnews01. [2000, May 2].

Kanter, R. M. (2001). *Evolve!: Succeeding in the digital culture of tomorrow.* Boston, MA: Harvard Business School Press.

Locker, K. (2000). *Business and administrative communications,* 5th ed. Boston, MA: Irwin-McGraw Hill.

MacPherson, K. (2000, February 14). Give them value . . . or nothing at all. *ClickZ Network.* www.clickz.com/cgi-bin/gt/fn/cz/cz.html? article=1312 [2000, February 14].

MacPherson, K. (2000, April 17). B2B discovers e-mail marketing. *ClickZ Network.* www.clickz.com/cgi-bin/gt/fn/emm/emm.html? article=1588 [1999, April 17].

McClean, C. (1999, January 12). E-mail: The phenomena you can't ignore in customer communications. *Pertinent Information.* www.pertinent.com/pertinfo/business/chrisCom2.html [1999, January 12].

McClean, C. (1999, January 12). How can e-mail communication affect your business? *E-mailtoday.com.* www.e-mailtoday.com/e-mailtoday/pr/e-mail_communication.htm [2000, January 12].

NUA. (2001, May 29). CRM key to profitability for online firms. *Nua Internet Surveys.* www.nua.ie/surveys [2001, June 6].

Ragan. (2000, March 9). Who is answering your e-mail? *RaganWeb.* www.ragan.com/newsletter/Article_WR_10705.html [2000, March 9].

Silverstein, B. (2000, March 10). E-fulfillment: Go there. *ClickZ Network.* www.clickz.com/cgi-bin/gt/fn/cz/cz.html? article=904 [2000, March 10].

Soukhanov, A. H. (Ed.). (1992). *The American heritage dictionary of the English language,* 3rd ed. Boston, MA: Houghton Mifflin Co.

Stemler, B. (2001, April 18). You want repeat customers? Try e-mail. *New York Times.* www.nytimes.com/2001/04/18/technology/18STAM.html [2001, April 23].

Tedeschi, B. (2001, May 28). E-Commerce report: Returns pose problem for e-tailers. *New York Times.* www.nytimes.com/2001/05/28/technology/28ECOMMERCE.html [2001, May 28].

Timm, P. H. (2001). *Customer service: Career success through customer service.* Upper Saddle River, NJ: Prentice Hall.

Usborne, N. (1999, February 22). More about writing e-mail. *ClickZ Network*. www. searchz.com/Articles/0222991.shtml [1999, February 22].

Usborne, N. (1999, August 6). Beware long brainload times. *ClickZ Network*. www. searchz.com/Articles/0806991.shtml [1999, August 6].

Usborne, N. (1999, November 15). Time to slow down. *ClickZ Network*. www. searchz. com/Articles/1115991.shtml [1999, November 15].

Usborne, N. (1999, November 29). How to be Human 101. ClickZ Network, www. clickz.com/cgi-bin/gt/cz/cz.html? article=3 [2000, June 7].

Usborne, N. (2001, September 20). Add more value to that automated e-mail. *ClickZ Network*. www. clickz.com/design/write-onl/article.php/887971 [2001, September 20].

Wayland, R. E. and Cole, P. M. (1997). *Customer connections: New strategies for growth.* Boston, MA: Harvard Business School Press.

Williams, K. (2000, March 10). Use e-mail to energize your customer service. R.R. Donnelley. www.ecommercetimes.com/news/ special_reports/customerservice.shtml [1999, October 15].

Wall Streel Journal. (1999, December 13). Frustrations grow over holiday e-tailing. *WSJ Interactive Edition*. www.zdnet.com/zdnn/stories/news/0,4586, 2408001,00.html [1999, December 13].

Zemke, R. and Connellan, T. (2000). *E-service: 24 ways to keep your customers—When the competition is just a click away.* New York, NY: AMACOM.

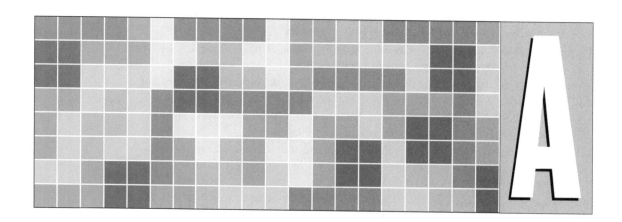

A Style Guide for E-mail: Standards for Effective E-mail Communications

"It is the quality of our work which will please God and not the quantity."

—Mahatma Gandhi

ASSESS YOUR E-MAIL QUOTIENT (EQ) FOR STYLE

Check ☑ *the following statements that describe your use of e-mail.*

1. ☐ Do you not know what punctuation to use after the greeting in an e-mail?

2. ☐ Do you not know how to format a list in an e-mail?

3. ☐ Did you ever write an e-mail without a greeting?

4. ☐ Have you ever sent an e-mail without signing it?

5. ☐ Do you not know how to be sure you have used parallel construction when your e-mail contains a list?

6. ☐ Do you not know how to format the title of a book in an e-mail?

7. ☐ Have you ever sent an e-mail with more than one attachment?

8. ☐ Do you omit your signature with your e-mail address and phone number?

9. ☐ Do you ever send e-mail that fills more than one screen, so the receiver has to scroll down to read it?

10. ☐ Do you ever send e-mail with all capital letters or with no capital letters?

If you placed a check next to three or more of these questions, you probably need some pointers on composing your e-mail.

Here begins your adventure of creating your e-mail style.

STANDARDIZING WHAT WE DO AT WORK IS ESSENTIAL

In many workplaces today, teams are working to standardize and document job tasks. Organizations have taken on this challenge for several reasons:

1. **To improve continuously.**

    Having standard operating procedures documented helps us define the steps we should follow to do job tasks. When we first document these tasks, we capture how we are functioning and can then take a critical look at the process and our job performance. We can then figure out how to improve both.

    Documenting and standardizing procedures is a key requirement of a quality initiative but is still a best practice of organizations that have not formally implemented one.

2. **To share knowledge.**

    Once we have work processes documented and refined, we can use this information to share knowledge. We can train new employees and cross-train or retrain existing employees. We can also educate vendors and customers about what happens in our work.

3. **To reinforce a positive brand image.**

    Organizations that are concerned with their brand image—who they are and what they stand for—want to be sure they have a handle on how things get done. Standardizing job tasks ensures the consistency in our work that contributes to a consistent and positive image.

Communicating through e-mail has become a *critical job task* of many employees. Even though many of us are working to improve other job tasks, we have yet to consider how to improve the way we communicate, especially through e-mail.

One way to improve our e-mail communications is to follow the *standards* outlined in this style guide. These standards have emerged from competent e-mail users who communicate in effective and responsible ways. Some of these standards are carried over from conventions in other forms of business writing: letters, memos, and reports. Other standards have appeared out of practicality. Because e-mail is a hybrid form of communication, many of the standards for communicating through e-mail are being created especially for this medium.

After examining thousands of e-mails, speaking with hundreds of e-mail users, and researching what has been written about e-mail communications to date, we are ready to share our knowledge with you. We suggest these standards to help you improve your e-mail communications. You can use this guide as another tool to help you continuously improve and reinforce a positive image for you and your organization by maintaining the professional style we have outlined in the following pages.

E-MAIL COMPOSED AT WORK SHOULD CONTAIN *STANDARD COMPONENTS*

To appear professional, to help you organize your thoughts, and to help your readers understand and act on your messages, you should include *standard components* in all your e-mails.

An e-mail is made up of five *components*: header, greeting, body, closing, and signature:

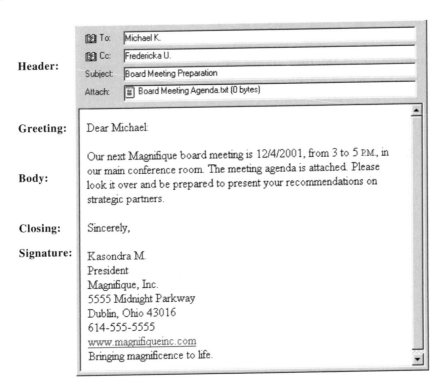

When you rush to send off your e-mails, especially if you are responding to a request or replying with a quick comment, you may be tempted to leave out information. You may even omit a component entirely. You may omit the greeting or you shoot off an e-mail with only the header filled in. You may leave out the signature or other important information.

What often happens as a result is that the reader, who could be receiving a flurry of e-mails, is caught off guard and may not remember what conversation is going on where. Not being present in the conversation can result in *mis*interpreting, *mis*understanding, or *mis*concluding. Recipients may not even know what they are expected to do.

Recipients may have to communicate with you again, have to look through previous messages, or in some other way have to refresh their memories and reconstruct the context of the message. A recipient may even choose to delete and *miss* the message altogether.

To avoid all these misses for you and recipients, include all of the components and make sure each of the components is complete, such as including a call for action within the body of the message. When you write an e-mail, always include and consciously compose:

1. A **subject line** that contains the essence of the message.

   A descriptive subject line is essential if you want recipients to read your message and act on it. Recipients who get lots of messages may delete and not even read e-mails if they cannot determine from the subject line that the message is important or relevant.

The subject line should be no longer than 10 words, should concisely yet precisely relay what the message is about, and reflect the stage or status of the conversation.

2. An **opening** or **greeting** or **salutation** that is friendly but businesslike and names the person you are addressing, such as:

   - Dear Mr. Wilson:
   - Amy,
   - Hello, Amy,

   To address a group of people without listing all their names use greetings such as:

   - Hello, All,
   - Good morning, Everyone,
   - Dear Team,

You may also use informal greetings depending on the purpose for writing and your relationship with the recipient. If you are writing to people you are familiar with, and you know a degree of informality is acceptable, you can use greetings such as:

   - Hi,
   - Greetings,

3. The **body**, which should make it easy for the recipient to jump in, connect, and converse. Be sure to include a:

   - **Context** or some background so the recipient can follow the thread of the conversation without having to do research or go back through previous messages or related materials.
   - **Complete explanation or answer** to each open question or concern.
   - **Call for action**, or *question* to be resolved, unless the e-mail is an acknowledgment of some other action.

4. A **closing** or **sign-off** to your message before you insert your signature, such as:

   - Regards,
   - Gratefully,
   - Good luck,
   - Thank you,
   - Sincerely,
   - All the best,

As with greetings, you may use informal closings depending on the purpose for writing and your relationship with the recipient. If you are writing to people you are familiar with, and you know a degree of informality is acceptable, you can use closings such as:

   - Cheers,
   - Later,

Or closings such as:

- Cheers,
- Later,

5. A **signature** that includes your *essential contact information*:
    - full name
    - title
    - business name
    - address
    - e-mail address
    - office phone number with area code plus extension
    - cell phone number
    - pager number
    - fax number
    - Web site

Your signature may also include a slogan, saying, or tag line that is part of your brand, such as:

Interactive Ink, Inc.
E-Business Made Easy

Including a proper and complete signature is essential so recipients of the message:

- know at first glance whom the message is from
- can reply in any medium (send a fax, call, etc.) without having to research your contact information
- can forward the message or print it and still have your contact information intact
- can refer to your e-mail later and not have to remember who sent it or how to contact you.

You can set up the signature in your e-mail software program to automatically appear whenever you compose a message. Your e-mail software may even allow you to create multiple signatures, so you can choose which one to use, depending on your audience.

In a threaded conversation, you may not need to include your full signature each time you respond, especially if you keep sending the messages in the thread intact. You may want to delete the full list of contact information and end your message with only your closing and name.

If the recipient knows you well, you may only have to include your name or an abbreviated signature that has only certain information, not all of it.

Remember, your name may be so different from your e-mail address that recipients may have no idea who you are (see table below).

Name	E-mail Address
Erica Smith	phishluvr@aol.com
Nancy Dean	NSDCoach@msn.com
Cliff Greenspan	Chester3@mindspring.com

You may also sign your name after the closing and before the automatic signature appears because:

- The recipient may know you by a nickname.
- You may wish to be more personal with the recipient, and adding just a first name before the signature helps strengthen the connection (see figure below).

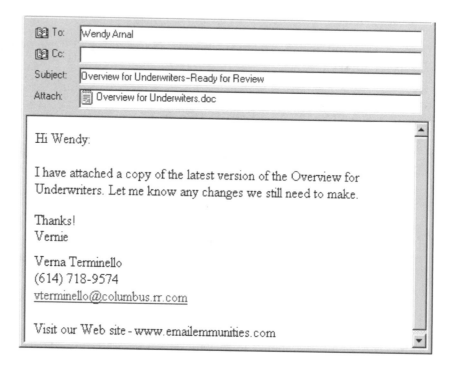

E-MAIL REQUIRES CORRECT *SPELLING*, AS DOES ANY FORMAL BUSINESS CORRESPONDENCE

You should learn a standard way for *spelling* words associated with the Internet and e-mail.

- *Internet* (always capitalize) or *Net*
- Web site (Write in two words, capitalize *Web*; do not capitalize *site*)

- *World Wide Web* or *WWW* unless used in a URL, such as www.prenhall.com

- *e-mail* We recommend using a hyphen in all *e* words where the *e* is for "electronic" to avoid confusion: *e-commerce, e-service, e-news, e-zine, e-world, e-billing*. The *e-* is easier to read and recognize as a prefix replacing the word, "electronic." When the hyphen is eliminated, the reader has to work harder to make the distinction between an *e-* word and a "regular" *e* word. A good business writer composes messages that are easy to read.

Standards are evolving for the e-world. We've seen *e-mail, email, eMail, E-Mail* and *Email*. Technical standards, as defined by the ASCII computer standards branch of the federal government, spell email as one word. This organization sets the standard for all software. Using this style is accepted by certain e-mmunities, but for business writing and to make your writing more readable, we recommend using the hyphen in the word e-mail.

New *e-* words and *m-* (replacing the word, "mobile," as in the word "mobile-learning or "m-learning") words are being created and added to the English language to characterize and note advances in technology and the explosion of information flying through cyberspace. However before these words are formally accepted in the lexicon as standard vocabulary, they must be around for a while, widely used, and tested.

Make sure you do not split your e words when they come at the end of a line, as indicated below:

> *"If every word or device that achievedcurrency were immediately authenticated, simply on the ground of popularity, the language would be as a ball game with no foul lines."*
> –Strunk & White, 2001

I enjoyed the newsletter, but I really liked when it became an e-zine.

Instead of

I enjoyed the newsletter, but I really liked when it became an e-zine.

You should learn a standard way for *spelling* words associated with the organization and industry you work for.

Always use your spell check before sending an e-mail. Remember, spelling counts if you want to:

- make sure your message is understood

- create a positive image of you and your organization

- establish credibility—that you are a reliable professional who pays attention to details.

Always check the spelling of your e-mail addresses. Messages have been returned or have disappeared in cyberspace because an address has been incorrectly spelled in the *To* line.

E-MAIL REQUIRES CORRECT *PUNCTUATION*, AS DOES ANY FORMAL BUSINESS CORRESPONDENCE

When you compose e-mail, you should keep in mind the *punctuation* rules that apply to any business correspondence.

We recommend using a style guide published by the American Psychological Association (APA), the Modern Language Association (MLA), or *The Chicago Manual of Style*. You could also refer to *The Elements of Style* by Strunk and White or a current grammar book, such as *The St. Martin's Handbook*, to find more information dealing with punctuation and usage rules.

In addition, pay attention to these simple punctuation rules that apply to e-mail:

- Use a colon (:) for a more formal, businesslike greeting, as in the greeting of a business letter.

- Use a comma (,) after the greeting if you know the recipient on a more friendly basis or after the first few times you have sent a person e-mails.

- Note: Some people use a dash (-) after the greeting, but it is a bit too informal. These choices are better:

  Dear Ms. Wilson:

  Hello, Ava Rose,

- Use a comma after the closing and add your name and/or signature on the lines below the closing.

  Sincerely,
  Roger

  Roger Jones
  VP Sales
  Jones Electric
  333 Warren St.
  Bergenfield, NJ 07621
  201-385-3653
  rj1@joneselectric.com

- Write in complete sentences unless you are writing a bulleted or numbered list. Make sure to end your sentences with periods or question marks. Sentences are easier to understand than phrases or fragments.

- Limit your use of exclamation points. Too many may make your message seem informal.

E-MAIL CAN BE *ORGANIZED* IN SEVERAL WAYS

Most e-mail messages should fit in one computer screen. Readers sometimes do not scroll down and do not pay attention to information below the first screen. Here are some ways to organize an e-mail.

1. One way to organize an e-mail message is to use a **modified inverted pyramid** style.

   - Write the most important information in the first line, like the lead in a news story, which contains the:
     - ☐ who
     - ☐ what
     - ☐ where
     - ☐ when
     - ☐ why
     - ☐ how
   - Put the smaller details in the next part of the message.
   - Write the call for action or question to be resolved as the last part of the message as follows:

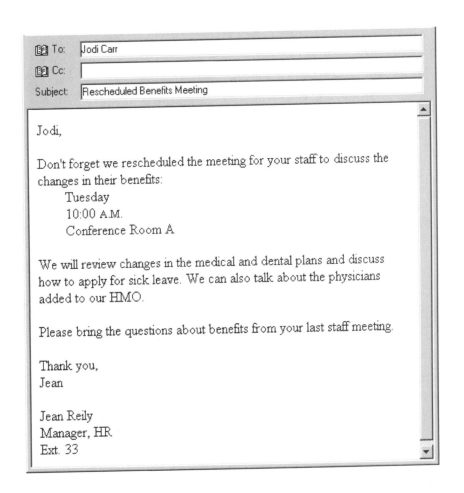

When composing e-mail, the modified inverted pyramid style works well because often readers pay most attention to the *beginning* and *end* of the message. So if the smaller details are important enough to include, but not essential to the action required as a result of the e-mail, then this style of organization should work efficiently.

2. Another way to organize an e-mail is **chronologically** or **sequentially**. This style is appropriate when your message relays either a
   - time sequence or
   - series of steps.

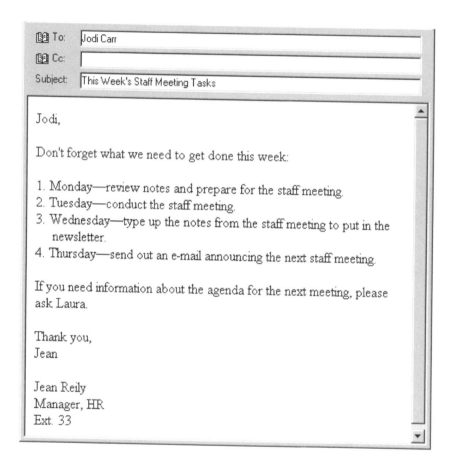

3. A third way to organize information is to write a **brief introductory message** and add the rest of the information in an **attachment** (see following figure). This organizational style is appropriate when you have:
   - too much information to fit in one screen
   - more than one or two short topics
   - longer information
   - information that is best displayed with formatting
   - a document beyond a simple message that the recipient might want to print

- information that the recipient may want to forward without the original e-mail
- information that recipients need to draft collaboratively—a working document

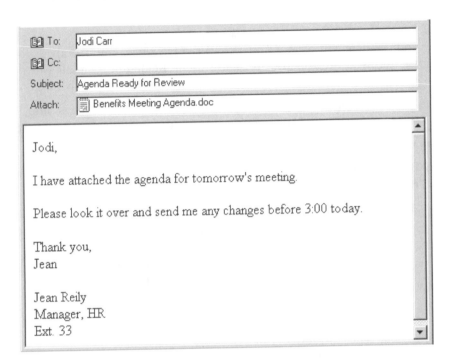

Note that the e-mail contains a reference to the attachment and ends with a call for action.

E-MAIL SHOULD CONTAIN SIMPLE, CONCISE, CORRECT, AND SENSITIVE *WORDING*

When composing an e-mail, think of your message as a fine gem. It is small, yet pure in form and valuable. Like a gem, your e-mail should contain only the essence—the most essential or more valuable part of some idea or experience. Your recipient should profit from receiving it and take actions that benefit both of you. One way to polish the gem is to be particular about the words you choose.

How we word e-mail messages, in addition to how long (or short) we make them, can help recipients read and act on them quickly.

E-mails should be composed with the following in mind:

- Use mostly present tense, active verbs (not passive) to relay a message around direct action.

    Say: *The committee usually plans the conference.* (active)

    Instead of: The conference is usually planned by the committee. (passive)

- Be concise. Eliminate unnecessary or complicated words. Use simple, straightforward language.

  Say: *I have attached the agenda for tomorrow's meeting.*

  Instead of: Attached please find the agenda for our meeting to be held tomorrow.

- Do not use abbreviations, acronyms, or jargon unless you are certain all your readers will clearly understand the reference. You can always define the terms if you feel you must use them. Remember, e-mails can be forwarded to or retrieved by people who do not know your business.

- Use correct, familiar words. Use words you know. Don't guess and try to use words that you think may make you sound intelligent or sophisticated.

- Make sure you use accurate times, dates, and numbers.

- Be sure to use correct, accurate, up-to-date titles of people you write to or refer to.

- Avoid using clichés, overused expressions, or business-speak.

  Say: *Please return the agenda with any changes.*

  Instead of: Please feel free to return the agenda with any cutting edge ideas you buy into and want me to shift my paradigm around.

- Use parallel forms for writing lists.

  If you use *verbs* to start a list, begin all items in the list with verbs in the same form:

  Say: The committee usually:

  - □ *plans* the conference
  - □ *brings* the food
  - □ *cleans* the room.

  Instead of: The committee usually:

  - □ plans the conference
  - □ has been bringing the food
  - □ cleaned the room.

  If you use *nouns* to start a list, begin all items in the list with nouns in the same form:

  Say: Please return the agenda with any *additions, corrections, or deletions.*

  Instead of: Please return the agenda with any additions, items corrected, or deleted.

- Avoid using sexist terms or inflammatory language. Never flame anyone!

  Say: Supervisors may bring a *guest.*

  Instead of: Supervisors may bring their wives.

- Be positive and use can-do language as much as you can; avoid negative words and expressions.

- Use transitions to give cohesion to your message. Sentences may begin with "and," "or," or "but." These words tie ideas together and help readers understand your message quickly.

■ Avoid using emoticons in business writing. (No smileys, frowns, or other symbols of emotion unless your brand is "playful," your customers will not think you are unprofessional, and they know what the emotions mean.) Occasional emoticons may be acceptable—but when you use them, you take the chance of annoying some people.

■ Use as many words as you can that describe and exemplify your brand when you communicate with external customers who you want to buy your products and services.

E-MAIL REQUIRES CERTAIN *FORMATTING* CONVENTIONS

■ Try to write your message so it fits in one computer screen. Recipients do not always scroll down to read the whole message if it is too long.

■ Use a font size easily read by most adults: 12–14 points is a good standard.

■ Format all e-mails in this standard style:
  ☐ Use a block style and begin paragraphs, greeting, and the closing flush left; do not indent them.
  ☐ Skip a line between the greeting and the body of the message.
  ☐ Use paragraphing and skip a line between paragraphs to help the reader skim through the message.
  ☐ Write the body in short paragraphs. One-sentence paragraphs are acceptable.
  ☐ Skip a line before the call to action paragraph.
  ☐ Skip a line before the closing.

■ List or bullet details so they are easy to pick out. You can also indent lists or details to help them stand out.

■ Use simple formatting because complex formatting may not appear correctly for all readers, who may use different e-mail and word processing software.
  ☐ Use keystrokes such as "*" or "-" to signal bullets instead of using the automatic bullet formats in some word processing software.
  ☐ Use asterisks to set off titles of works or to replace italics in e-mail.
    Use: *E-mail: Communicate Effectively*
    Instead of: *E-mail: Communicate Effectively*
  ☐ Use highlighting devices such as bold, italics, borders, special or colored fonts only if you know your recipient has the software to read these.

■ Keep the number of characters per line below 80. Longer lines may appear choppy in some recipient's messages. We never know where the recipients' software might break a line of text. Your recipient will have a hard time reading a message that is chopped up in strange places.

■ Use upper- and lower-case letters in e-mail messages. Using all capital letters is usually seen as shouting and is too difficult to read.

■ Double space after punctuation that ends a sentence. The double space helps readers keep their place while reading on a computer screen.

- Write addresses within an e-mail by separating the lines in the message as they would appear on an envelope.

- Remember: white space is a good thing.

References

Angell, D. and Heslop, B. (1994). *The elements of e-mail style*. Reading: Addison-Wesley Publishing Company.

McGovern, G. (2001, July 5). The text revolution. *ClickZ*, www.clickz.com/article/cz.4077.html [2001, July 5].

Strunk, W. and White, E. B. (2000). *The Elements of Style*. Boston, MA: Allyn & Bacon.

Answers for Quick Checks

CHAPTER 1 QUICK CHECK ANSWERS

1. True

2. False

3. a) Can be composed or read when user has time
   b) Can reduce telephone tag
   c) Can stay in mailbox as reminders

4. Voices, gestures, pauses, and other nonverbal cues are lost.

5. False

6. False

7. False

8. Electronic community

9. True

10. The tone could be misinterpreted as criticism or harsh words.

CHAPTER 2 QUICK CHECK ANSWERS

1. d
2. False
3. Flames
4. Spam
5. Jam
6. True
7. False
8. False
9. True
10. All recipients may not understand them clearly or quickly

CHAPTER 3 QUICK CHECK ANSWERS

1. False
2. Mapping, brainstorming, outlining, free writing
3. Capture the essence of your message in as few words as possible and capture the receiver's attention so the message will be read
4. True
5. True
6. Clear, concise, correct, conscious, complete, considerate, courteous, consistent, concrete, and connecting
7. False
8. Anyone to whom the message is copied
9. To introduce any news that may be considered controversial
10. False

CHAPTER 4 QUICK CHECK ANSWERS

1. Protocol

2. Organizing, processing, and decluttering

3. Scan, skim, study, sort

4. Delete, delegate, do now, delay, dock

5. True

6. Scan to find out who the message is from, what the subject is, and when the message was sent. Skim to find out why the message was sent.

7. Limit the inflow, keep things moving, limit the outflow, put things where they belong, consolidate, filter, purge

8. True

9. True

10. False

CHAPTER 5 QUICK CHECK ANSWERS

1. True

2. False

3. Heart and soul, or personalization

4. Have someone else (preferably your e-mail buddy) read and help revise your e-mail

5. So your customer can contact you easily, without researching your contact information

6. So your customer can call you on the phone if they prefer voice contact

7. Because customers must be *more* than satisfied to become loyal partners or advocates

8. To make up for the frustration, time, and effort the customers put into getting their problem resolved—this builds trust that you value them and are doing your best to make their lives easier

9. So you can make sure your communication is effective, responsible, and correct and so you can anticipate any questions or issues they may have

10. To project your organization's desired image and to build trust. Customers trust organizations and people who are consistent in their communications

Suggested Answers for Activities

Below is our suggested map for canceling an order.

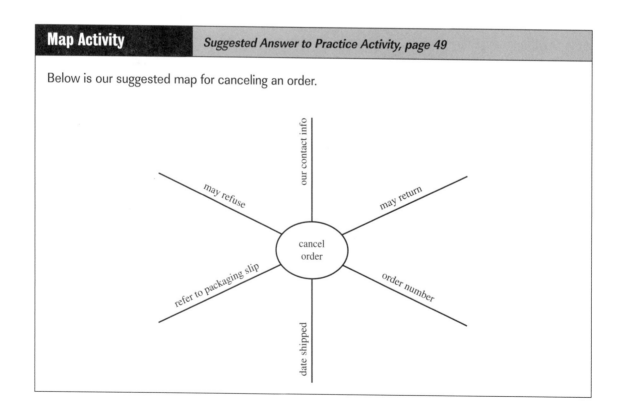

Brainstorm Activity   *Suggested Answer to Practice Activity, page 51*

Below is our suggested brainstorm for canceling an order.

Cancel order

- Unable to cancel order
- Order number
- Date of shipment
- Refer to packing ship
- May refuse shipment
- May return order

Outline Activity   *Suggested Answer to Practice Activity, page 53*

Below is our suggested outline for canceling an order.

Cancel order

who: we

what: unable to cancel order number

where: packing slip for policy and instructions or use Web site

when: when order arrives

why: shipment already sent on date

how: may return order or refuse shipment

Free Write Activity   *Suggested Answer to Practice Activity, page 54*

Below is our suggested free write for canceling an order.

Cancel order

We were unable to cancel your order number shipped on—. The packing slip has instructions for sending back the order if you do not want it. Or you can use the Web site. When the order arrives you may refuse shipment or you may return the order. The order was already sent on—.

Glossary of Terms

acknowledgment—a response that either lets the sender know you received the message or you understand the message and care

acronym—a shorthand method of communicating by using the first letter of each word in a phrase. Acronyms are used frequently in electronic communications; for example, IMHO means "in my humble opinion."

attachments—one or more files you attach to an e-mail message. The attachment can be a word processing file, a spreadsheet, a database, a picture or graphic, an html page, or other file your recipient can read.

audience—the recipient(s) or potential recipient(s) of your message

autoresponse—automated e-mail responses generated by a computer (software) in response to customer actions

bandwidth—the amount of information that can be transmitted across a connection

bulletin board—an electronic message system for reading and posting messages

business speak—old, worn-out phrases traditionally used in business correspondence to make the writer sound professional and businesslike

chat room—a virtual "room" where users can "talk" live with each other through electronic messages

complaint site—Web sites where consumers can register complaints with a service provider online

compose—use a process to write

contact management—the process of managing, tracking, and organizing contacts with your prospective and existing customers.

context—background or connecting information

customer relationship management (CRM)—a set of customer-centric strategies relating to policies, processes, applications, and people positioned to manage and increase profitable relationships with customers. All functional areas are involved, including sales, marketing, customer service, finance and accounting, production, scheduling, inventory, and shipping.

cyberspace—the Internet and its available set of services

database—information that has been captured and saved so it can be easily retrieved and used

draft—the part of the writing process during which you put together the message

e-commerce—business conducted on the Internet

e-lingo—electronic jargon

e-mail—electronic mail

e-mmunity—electronic community

emoticon—an e-mail symbol that represents emotion

e-service—using electronic communications to stay in touch with your customers, whether using a sophisticated CRM system or simply by adding e-mail to your customer communications

e-signature—see *signature*

fatty file—a large file attachment, so large that it may not transfer without causing problems

flame—a nasty-gram; an e-mail shouting match; see *nasty-gram*

formatting—using highlighting devices such as bullets or numbering or white space to help make the document readable

jam—unsolicited junk e-mail from someone the recipient knows

knowledge base—classified, codified, and organized knowledge that is the result of a knowledge management system

knowledge management—ways to create, identify, capture, and share organizational knowledge with the people who need it

listserv—programs that automatically manage and distribute messages to e-mail lists

mission critical—central, important to the mission and business goals of the organization

nasty-gram—a mean or nasty note or e-mail message; see *flame*

Netiquette—etiquette for the Internet

Netizen—Internet citizen

newsgroup—an electronic bulletin board where users post messages that can be read and replied to by other members of the group

opt in—choose to receive e-mail or other communications from a service provider

paper trail—written documentation that can help reconstruct an event or series of events

personalization—customizing an e-mail message to a customer based on the customer's profile, purchases, or their last communication. The personalized message is composed or modified to meet the customer's psychological and product/service needs.

reading-to-do—reading to determine the actions required to fulfill your goals or purpose

reading-to-learn—reading to remember information that we may retrieve at another time

Rolodex—the brand name by Eldon for address or business cards stored on an office desk in rotary files or tray files. Electronic versions of Rolodex cards are also available.

shortness syndrome—leaving out important information in a written message (i.e., not providing context in an e-mail message)

signature—contact information at the end of your e-mail that could include name, organization, title, address, phone number with extension, Web site address, and e-mail address. (Many e-mailers assume the recipient knows who they are and how to contact them. Providing a complete signature makes it easy for the recipient to reach you.)

spam—unsolicited junk e-mail from someone unknown to the recipient

template—a standard form letter used as a guide for composing effective e-mail communications

threaded conversation—an ongoing electronic conversation on a specific discussion subject

Index